IMAGES OF CUMBRIAN RAILWAYS

JOHN MARSH & JOHN GARBUTT

Sutton Publishing Limited
Phoenix Mill · Thrupp · Stroud
Gloucestershire · GL5 2BU

First published 2002

Half-title page photograph: LMS No. 5568 *Western Australia* with Thames Forth express near Aisgill on the Settle to Carlisle line.

Below: The authors (Garbutt left, Marsh right) at the launch of *Cumbrian Railways* at Kendal Library, 1999.

Opposite: LMS Royal Scot No. 6147 *The Northamptonshire Regiment* on the Windermere branch platform at Oxenholme *c*. 1960.

British Library Cataloguing in Publication Data
A catalogue record for this book is available from the British Library.

ISBN 0-7509-2834-4

Typeset in 10.5/13.5 Photina.
Typesetting and origination by
Sutton Publishing Limited.
Printed and bound in England by
J.H. Haynes & Co. Ltd, Sparkford.

> *This book is dedicated to Preston Whiteley, rail enthusiast, who again has helped with provision of material and generous advice.*

IMAGES OF CUMBRIAN RAILWAYS

JOHN MARSH & JOHN GARBUTT

SUTTON PUBLISHING

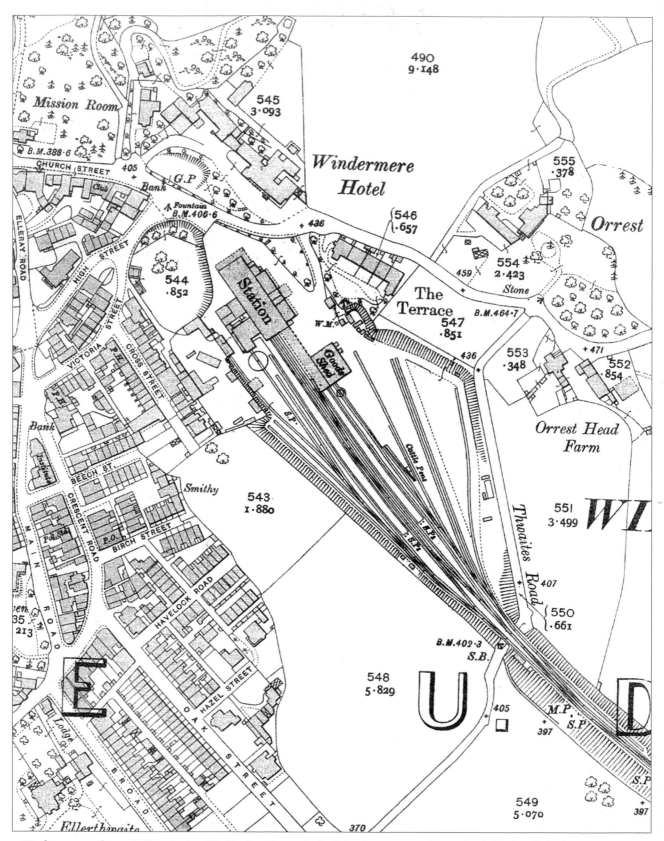

Windermere railway station site in 1912 before the arrival of Booths supermarket and Lakeland Ltd. (Ordnance Survey)

CONTENTS

Note: The authors have included material from all the Cumbrian Railway lines in Vol. 1 using photographic illustrations and archive material. The material available for Vol. 2 did not offer this complete coverage and thus the contents listed above generally follow the format of Vol. 1 but not in every detail, as a comparison will show. Nevertheless, we feel this second range of material gives a more complete picture of Cumbrian Railways by adding to the wide coverage of Vol. 1 and we suggest both books are used together.

Torver Crossing on the Furness Railway Coniston branch in the 1930s with Tom Coward, Foreman Platelayer and smallholding farmer who, unfortunately, was killed by his pet bull. (J. Kitchin)

INTRODUCTION

The publication of the authors' first book on the railways of Cumbria – *Cumbrian Railways* (Suttons 1999) – caused much excited comment and critical acclaim at the time of publication. The book sold well in all parts of the county of Cumbria and elsewhere and prompted comments from home and abroad as most of the photographs had never been seen before. This acclaim was continued into the Cumbria Book of the Year Awards 2000 where *Cumbrian Railways* was highly commended in the Tullie House category for the best environmental and social book. The authors were only too aware that they had had to leave out of their book much other unpublished material in their own and other collections; and, as word of that got about, pressure was put on them to publish a second book of Cumbrian Railways material – and here it is. *Images of Cumbrian Railways* brings together another collection of mostly unpublished material that is certain to excite railway enthusiasts and anyone else interested in the visual history of a county railway system now generally lost to the pressures of a national railway network.

The authors have been interested in the subject since, as boys at Ulverston Grammar School in the 1940s, they were founding members of the school Local History Society. This was wartime when the railways were the main form of transport but it was becoming obvious that systems were already getting past their best and were on the long decline that was outlined in the previous volume, *Cumbrian Railways*. Collecting old photographs and other archive material became a post-retirement hobby for both authors when it was soon realised that much of the material was unique and deserved publication. Neither of the books pretends to be a formal history book as they were designed to present to the public and historians much material that had never been seen before and thus further the study of local railway history. There is also much nostalgia to please a wider readership.

In Ulverston the comings and goings on the railway in wartime had to be experienced to be believed. So many young men went off from the platforms at the station never to be seen again. Mysterious well-covered material went towards Barrow-in-Furness and, as D-Day approached, endless covered trains of tanks and guns that had been stored in the lanes surrounding Barrow and Ulverston went off to war. It was exciting for young boys but deadly serious for almost everybody else. In our book we include photographs of young men going off to the front from other railway stations in Cumbria for an earlier war. It is obvious from their eager young faces that they had no idea what the Generals of both sides had in mind for them. By 1914, except for a short sea passage, many went from local stations in Cumbria straight to the slaughter, travelling all the way by railway; their home at one end of the track and their grave at the other. In our turn in the 1950s both authors went off down the track for their national service, one to wartorn Germany and the other to Manchester, which in those days had many barracks and still bore the traces of German bombing. The war was over but the railways looked tired and worn out by the war years. Stations carried huge notices, 'Air Raid Shelter', 'Fire Post' and 'Air Raid Warden' as the economy that saw the railways deteriorate did not allow for their removal. The engines and rolling stock became dilapidated, a condition that even the takeover of the railway companies by government to form British Rail, could not stop. New engines appeared but soon became dirty and tired looking. The railways were on a very steep decline and their value was not fully realised until many lines had been swept away by dogma-led politicians and narrow-minded accountants. So thus we have today 'restoration groups' begging for millions of pounds to replace railway systems destroyed only decades before by shortsighted policies that not only destroyed railways but also contaminated Cumbria's towns and villages with motor transport. We can but wish these restoration groups well in their endeavours and hope our collections of pictures of how things used to be might help their cause.

We wish to acknowledge the assistance given to us by Preston Whiteley, who again has freely let us use his material, Mrs G. Carrick of Kendal, George Dawson of Kendal, who has again produced material from his extensive archive, Jackie Fay of the Cumbria Library service, Kendal Public Library, which organised the book launch of *Cumbria Railways* in May 1999 and which has assisted in the production of this volume, Mr W. Barrow, Mr D. Hinde of Brigham and Neville Stead of Whitley Bay, where the range and quality of his collection never ceases to amaze us. We also wish to thank all the readers of the 1999 book who wrote to us from many parts of the world to encourage our efforts and add material we would not otherwise have been aware of. It would appear that many specific histories of parts of the Cumbrian Railway system await publication and we look forward to their appearance aided, possibly, by our two volumes on Cumbrian Railways.

John Marsh & John Garbutt
Spring 2002

1

The London & North Western Railway

LNWR Webb 2–4–0 on the line from the south into Cumbria, *c.* 1910. The last of this class of engine, which did sterling service for the LNWR for many decades, was withdrawn by the LMS in the 1930s. (J. Marsh collection)

Nowadays called the West Coast Main Line, this line connected with the Caledonian Railway to provide the first through route from the capital to Scotland in 1848. The east coast railway followed two years later and thus started the many decades of competition between the two routes and much celebration of achievement (*see* page 23). The Midland Railway had great difficulty in achieving a main line to Scotland until later years as much depended on routes provided by other companies. Not until 1923, when the London Midland and Scottish Railway Company absorbed the London & North Western Railway, the Midland Railway and the Caledonian Railway, was the battle between the smaller companies for routes fully resolved. As shown in Book 1, the LNWR had very useful junctions in Cumbria with the Furness Railway, the Eastern Railway, the Cockermouth, Keswick and Penrith Railway and the many west coast lines through the Maryport and Carlisle Railway, and soon became the senior partner in managing traffic through those junctions. The London Midland and Scottish Railway became part of British Rail in 1948. Steam power was withdrawn in favour of diesel twenty years later and the system was electrified in the 1970s. Railway towns and villages grew around the junctions and where the railway touched existing market towns these also grew. Oxenholme (or Kendal junction) became a small railway village where no village had existed previously. Tebay expanded from a few houses to a large village with a railway church and club, hotels and a police station. Penrith, a prosperous market town, grew with the addition of housing for the railway workers and hotel accommodation for the travellers. Carlisle saw the largest expansion on the old LNWR route to the north. Already a Cathedral city, many parts of modern Carlisle appeared as a direct result of housing the railway workers who were employed in either the city centre Citadel station or one of a number of railway depots that surrounded the centre, some of which had started life as not only depots but also stations for one of the railway companies anxious for a connection in the town.

Arnside Viaduct, 23 May 1976, when ex-LNWR 2–4–0 No. 790 *Hardwicke* pulled a special train from Carnforth to Grange-over-Sands. Built at Crewe in 1873, *Hardwicke* was one of a series of engines that hauled main line expresses for the LNWR through Cumbria for many decades and it took part in the famous 1895 race to Scotland. Taken over by the LMS in 1923 and given the number 5031, it was withdrawn in 1932 to end up in the Crewe railway workshop paint shop repainted in the original LNWR colour scheme. After preservation in the Clapham Transport Museum it was moved to the National Railway Museum at York where it can be seen today. (N. Stead)

Hilderstone, near Burton-in-Kendal, was where the LNWR left Lancashire and entered Cumbria. This photograph from 1910 shows how well kept the railway line was in those days with nicely cut grass verges and hedges. (Mrs Rowbotham, J. Marsh collection)

Burton-in-Kendal station, *c.* 1910, when volunteers with the Royal Field Artillery had just detrained in the siding and were reassembling outside the Station Hotel before making their way to the camp field by the canal at Farleton. Many volunteer training camps were held in the years just before the First World War and most servicemen travelled to their camps by railway. (*See also* page 5) (Mrs Rowbotham)

The Gatebeck horse-drawn tramway in 1933/4 with Wadeson Barrow sitting in front of a wagon containing 4 tons 10 cwt of explosives. By that time the gunpowder works was owned by ICI and would be closed, along with the tramway, in a few years. (W. Barrow collection)

The tramway from Gatebeck to Milnthorpe station was built to convey gunpowder from the Gatebeck works to a special warehouse at Milnthorpe where the transfer took place of the explosives from the tramway wagon to LNWR special vans. The tramway was constructed in 1875 and part of the route, with agreement with the canal company (part of the LNWR), was over the Lancaster to Kendal canal at Crooklands. By the 1930s, it is reported, the tramway bridge became so rickety that drivers walked across the adjoining road bridge leaving the horse to pull the wagon on the lines! The tramway bridge is seen in the photograph in the 1920s with the Crooklands canal bridge behind. (J. Marsh collection)

Oxenholme railway station saw much military coming and going in the years leading up to the First World War. Here a group of Territorials are lined up on the road prior to marching to either Holmescales camp or to Longlands camp in Kendal. (J. Marsh collection)

Oxenholme station from the road bridge before the First World War showing the goods sidings and the Kendal and Windermere branch on the left. (Simcoe and Son, J. Marsh collection)

Royal Scot class 7P No. 46142 *The York and Lancaster Regiment* waits by the water tower at Oxenholme giving the driver a chance for a chat. These magnificent engines were a regular sight on passenger trains at Oxenholme in the postwar years. Originating with the LMS in 1927 many at first had a parallel boiler (*see* page iii) to be later replaced with the sloping boiler seen here. (P. Whiteley)

Coaches at Kendal railway station, *c.* 1914. Three coaches wait for passengers from the train. The local hotels picked up many clients in this way and many travellers booked a coach to meet them as part of the railway journey arrangements. (G. Dawson collection)

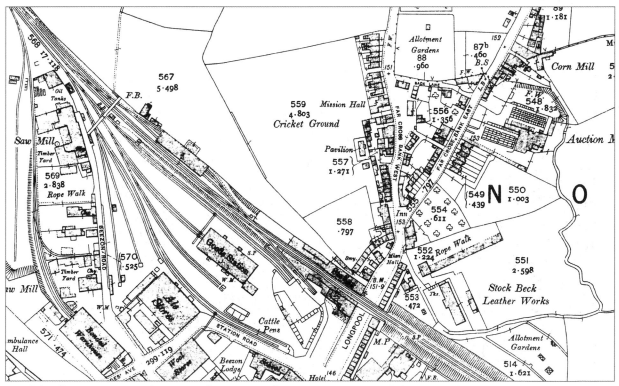

Kendal railway station as shown on the 1914 Ordnance Survey map of the town. This is a much changed scene today. The Wool stores is now the Kendal Museum (note the extra line into the stores from the goods yard at Station Road). The goods yard is now the site of many local businesses and the cattle pens are no more. (Ordnance Survey)

Kendal railway station. A crowd waits on the southbound platform with an LNWR third-class coach in the background. One can but presume that the picture is of the party rather than of the station but unfortunately no information came with the old slide from which this picture was taken. (J. Marsh collection)

Kendal railway station goods yard in the days of the construction of the Manchester Corporation water pipeline from Thirlmere to Manchester. The steam wagon was owned by Charles Cumpstey and the driver was Jack Kellett. (J. Marsh collection)

Staveley level crossing in 1905 with a horse and carriage posed for the picture and two LNWR employees anxiously observing the scene. The Brunskill family of Kendal used the photograph as a Christmas card that year. (Photo: Ashworth of Kendal) (J. Marsh collection)

Windermere railway station, *c.* 1910. This was meant to be a through station on a route to Ambleside, and maybe beyond, but the original intentions were never achieved. It was also to be a junction to Ulverston – *see* page 140 – but that line through Storrs was never built. The fine water fountain can now be seen in the grounds of the Kendal Brewery Arts Centre. (Britain & Wright, J. Marsh collection)

Elterwater Gun Powder works in Langdale exported its products via the London and North Western Railway station at Windermere. The first part of the journey was on horse-drawn carts which were well spaced out on their very bumpy trip on the unmade roads of the day. The annual parade of the horses on May Day was photographed in 1907 with some of the gunpowder workers posed behind. (J. Marsh collection)

Windermere railway station interior, platform two, with Wyman's bookstall, its advertising for newspapers and its own library. A supermarket now stands on the site. (J. Marsh collection)

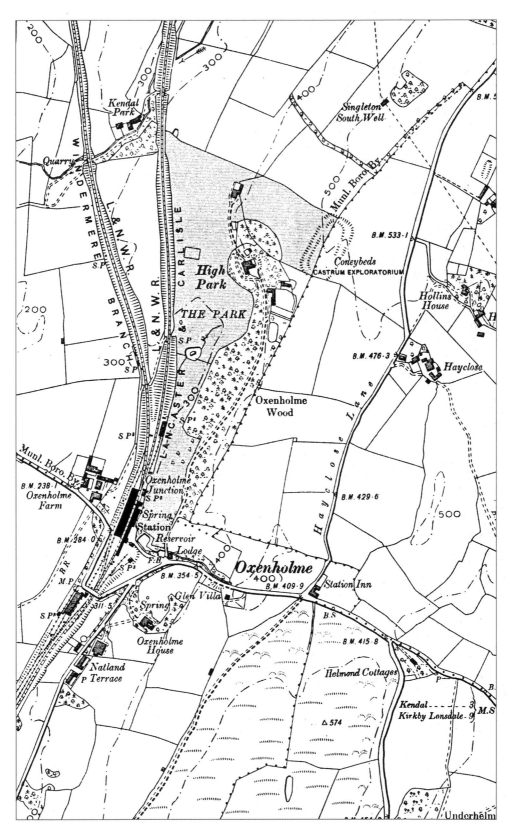

Oxenholme railway station showing the junction with the Windermere line as it appeared on the 1899 Ordnance Survey map. (Ordnance Survey)

Oxenholme station, August 1965, when Britannia class 4–6–2 No. 70040 roared through the station with an express goods train. The end of steam was near and the thieving of engine parts which took place at the time is attested by the missing nameplate from the side shield. The plate would have read *Clive of India*. These huge engines were introduced by engineer R.A. Riddles to British Rail in 1951 but the end of steam in 1968 ended what was intended to be a huge production run. Nos 70000 *Britannia* and 70013 *Oliver Cromwell* were immediately preserved and did not face the scrapheap, as did the majority of this short-lived class. (Alexandra, P. Whiteley collection)

The down line towards Shap at Oxenholme in summer 1966 with Stanier 8F 2–8–0 No. 48151 pulling a mixed goods northwards. Introduced by the LMS in 1935, many of this class of engine went straight into war service in 1939. In all, 849 engines were reported to have been built. (P. Whiteley)

Above: Dillicar Troughs south of Shap station was where many nonstop trains picked up water by lowering a scoop into the water troughs. Here Furness railway 0–6–0 No. 32 is pulling a Durham Coke train sometime before 1924. Any waiting enthusiasts would have been disappointed as the engine did not use the troughs. Furness railway engine No. 32 was built in 1920 and scrapped as No. 12509 by British Rail in 1956. (J. Marsh collection)

Coronation Scot on Dillicar Troughs is a photographers' dream which was fulfilled in the late 1930s by the Valentine's of Dundee photographer for their postcard series. Sir William Stanier's design was tested to the full in the years before the Second World War and in 1937 No. 46220 achieved 114 miles per hour. These engines were the pride of the LMS for a number of years and in the days of British Rail were given an extra 4 in front of their LMS number. (G. Dawson collection)

The Royal Scot was another LMS famous express and, again, to catch the train on Dillicar Troughs was considered rather good by train spotters. In this earlier 1930s shot for Valentine's postcards, the photographer pulled a double success as the engine on the train was the class leader No. 6100 (B.R. No. 46100). This 137-ton engine toured the USA in 1933 and the bell which was presented to the engine on that tour can be seen above the front buffer beam. (J. Marsh collection)

Tebay station on 16 June 1963 with English Electric class 40 No. D287 running south with the 4.13 pm Carlisle to Preston 'local' through the soon-to-be-demolished station. In the background are the signal box and the Kirkby Stephen branch line. (*See also* the top picture on page 124 of our 1999 book). Times were rapidly changing in both rolling stock and station at Tebay. (P. Whiteley collection)

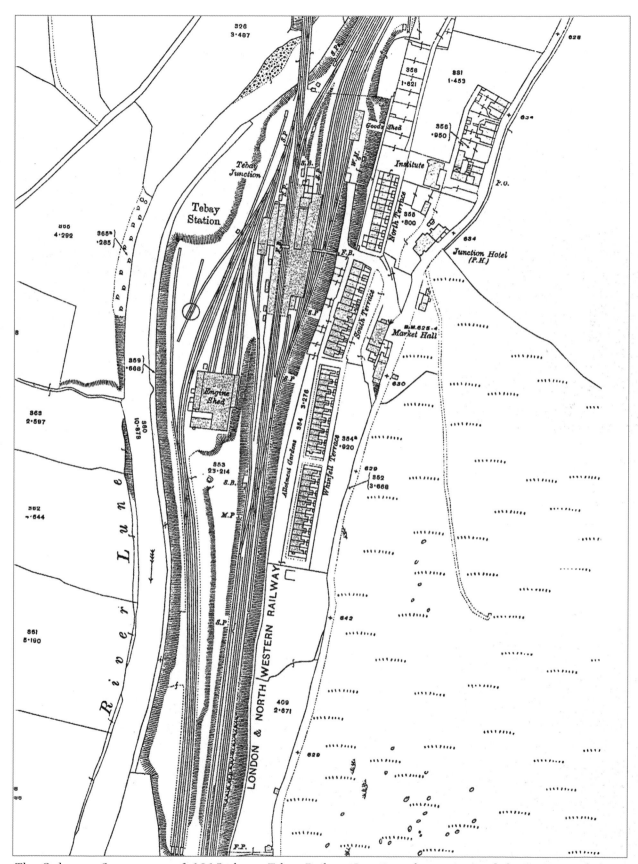

The Ordnance Survey map of 1915 shows Tebay Railway Junction, the station and depot. None of these remains. (*See* page 18) (Kendal Library collection)

The site of Tebay railway station in 1998 with the West Coast main line running through the centre of the picture. There is no station and no junction here anymore and the railway villagers have found other ways of making a living. (J. Marsh)

Tebay junction with the NE line running away on the right, 24 June 1961. Royal Scot class 4–6–0 express engine No. 46104 *Scottish Borderer* brings a southbound passenger train towards Tebay station from Carlisle and the north. (P.B. Booth, N. Stead collection)

Tebay sheds in the 1960s with a fine collection of engines to be seen. Monster 2–10–0 freight engine No. 92218 is in the centre with mixed traffic 4–6–0 No. 75037 inside the shed. Both of these engines were introduced in the 1950s and neither, like the shed, would survive the great changes being planned as the picture was being taken. (*See also* page 109) (N. Stead collection)

Shap Bank on the main line north of Tebay with 2–6–0 mixed traffic engine No. 77014 pulling a tracklaying work train north, 21 June 1962. Introduced by British Rail in 1954 for work in the north of England and Scotland they were called 'an ugly engine', which is possibly why none are recorded as being preserved. (P. Whiteley collection)

Near Shap summit with the quarry siding nearby on Boxing Day 1967. Now preserved Britannia class 4–6–2 No. 70013 *Oliver Cromwell* in fine form with a football special from Carlisle to Blackpool. 70013 was the last steam engine to be fully restored by British Railways and ran until August 1968 when it was sold for preservation. (N. Stead collection)

Shap with Black Five 4–6–0 No. 45326 hauling a mixed goods train on 21 September 1961. This class of engine proved popular for preservation, as it had been in its working days a reliable and useful design. Sir William Stanier's 1934 design, which was similar to the Jubilee class but smaller in a number of ways, lived on in Cumbria on the Lakeside & Haverthwaite Railway which purchased five for their holiday line between Haverthwaite and Lake Windermere. (P. Whiteley collection)

Shap station in the 1960s, about the time of its closure, with Royal Scot class 4–6–0 No. 46115 *Scots Guardsman* pulling away with a passenger train. (N. Stead collection)

Penrith station with a busy view on 27 July 1963 as the 10.15 am Manchester to Keswick train is about to pull away, hauled by Mogul class 2–6–0 No. 46410. (*See also* our 1999 book for more of this class on the CK & P line). (P. Whiteley collection)

Near Wreay an ex-London and North Western 0–8–0 is photographed in full steam at the head of a southbound goods train, *c.* 1937. These engines were designed by C.J. Bowen-Cooke in 1912 for the LNWR and the last was withdrawn from BR service in 1964. The engine in the picture is LMS No. 9196 which had previously been LNWR No. 2091. (N. Stead collection)

Upperby depot on 13 April 1965 when Royal Scot class 4–6–0 No. 46115 *Scots Guardsman* (*see also* page 21) gets steam up to take a rail special. One of Preston Whiteley's pictures of this event carries the words 'good external condition' as though there were internal problems. (P. Whiteley)

Upperby depot, Carlisle with ex-LMS Mogul 2–6–0 No. 46426 doing a little shunting, 25 June 1966. These Ivatt-designed engines appeared in 1946 in the last years of the LMS railway and were used widely by British Rail who constructed over 100 more of this useful workhorse. No. 46441 of this class is preserved on the Lakeside & haverthewaite railway in Cumbria. (P. Whiteley)

Special postcards were issued by the LNWR when on 19 July 1903 a special train ran non-stop from London to Carlisle, a distance of 299 miles. Postcard collectors and train enthusiasts added to the rush to buy these advertising cards which all railway companies issued in one form or another. (J. Marsh collection)

Carlisle Citadel station in two early twentieth-century views. Above, John Menzies bookstall has a more permanent appearance than it did on page 32 of our 1999 *Cumbrian Railways* book. Left, the scene outside the station and The Courts where horse carriages ply for what must have been a busy passing trade. (both pictures J. Marsh collection)

George Stephenson appeared on another of the LNWR's series of postcards. The 'Father of Railways' had favoured the west coast route over Morecambe Bay and the Duddon sands and was the first engineer of the Maryport and Carlisle railway and the Whitehaven Junction Railway. (J. Marsh collection)

Kingmoor, Carlisle and the changing scene in the twentieth century. Above, a 4–6–2 Princess Coronation class 8P No. 46237 *City of Bristol* is getting up steam, 22 July 1961; below, before amalgamation, Caledonian Railway engines stand, all under steam, as a complete contrast in steam locomotion. These Caledonian Railway McIntosh Dunalastair class 2P locos were being passed on to the London Midland and Scottish Railway in 1923 to be renumbered 14311 to 14336. Built in 1896–7, all were withdrawn by 1948. (Top photo: P. Whiteley. Bottom: J. Marsh collection)

Kingmoor was a popular place for train buffs in the 1960s. In Carlisle all was changing and the end of steam was near. Two photographs by Preston Whiteley show (above) the scene on 20 July 1960 when Clan class 4–6–2 No. 72002 *Clan Campbell* was parked up in the Kingmoor yard. A year later Preston Whiteley was again at Kingmoor to photograph the magnificent Princess Coronation class 4–6–2 No. 46224 below, which was named after the North West's own Princess Alexandra. Neither the *City of Carlisle* (*see* page 150 and also page 9 of our 1999 *Cumbrian Railways* book), nor the *Princess Alexandra* seems to have caught the imagination of Cumbrians when their turn came for scrapping, leaving us now pondering on the lost opportunities. (P. Whiteley)

Approaching Kingmoor on 17 September 1966 was class 5 MT 4–6–0 No. 44802 with a train of empty hoppers. These 125-ton workhorses were introduced on the LMS railway in the 1930s by Sir William Stanier. (P. Whiteley)

Dentonholme was to become the remaining goods depot for Carlisle after the Beeching cuts of the 1960s/70s but all that was in the future when the ex-North British 0–6–2 N-15 class locomotive No. 69155 was photographed with a very 'mixed goods' train on 19 September 1959. Designed by W.P. Reid for the North British Railway in 1910, its size and use as a shunting engine ensured its long life into British Rail days. (G.M. Staddon, N. Stead collection)

2

The Midland Railway

Royal Scot class 4–6–0 No. 46113 *Cameronian* takes the southbound Thames–Clyde express out of Mallerstang towards Aisgill in 1961. First introduced in 1927 by the North British Loco. Co. for the LMS, in April 1928 this engine, No. 46113 had gained fame by taking an express train the 401.5 miles from Euston to Glasgow non-stop, in those days a world record run. (N. Stead collection)

Aisgill summit on the Settle to Carlisle railway with ex-LNER main line A-3 Pacific No. 60086 *Gainsborough* taking a northbound express out of Yorkshire into Cumbria in May 1961. Introduced in 1922 for the East Coast main line by Sir Nigel Gresley these engines in BR days made light work of the Leeds to Carlisle route on which Aisgill was the highest point. (Photo: P.B. Booth) (N. Stead collection)

Right: Aisgill road bridge, May 1961, when an ex-War Department class engine No. 90012 designed by R.A. Riddles in 1943 as a long-distance freight engine can be seen on a Leeds-bound express freight train. These engines were sold to the LNER after the war, and later to British Railways. Hundreds were built and were common in the county until steam power was replaced in 1968. (N. Stead collection)

A few miles along the Ingleton road below the famous viaduct at Ribblehead is the tiny church of Chapel-le-Dale where many who were killed while employed on the construction of the Settle to Carlisle railway through the Pennines from Yorkshire into Cumbria are buried. There are few memorials in the graveyard but inside the church on the west wall is this memorial 'erected at the expense of their fellow workmen and the Midland Rilway Company'. The section of line between Ribblehead and Denthead included the Blea Moor tunnel where many lives were lost. In 1869 all of the line to Aisgill summit was in Yorkshire but since 1974 the boundary has been at Denthead. (J. Marsh)

Hughes-Fowler 2–6–0 No. 42883 climbs out of Mallerstang towards Aisgill with a southbound parcels train on 24 April 1962. These magnificent 'mixed traffic' engines were introduced on to the LMS in 1926 and given 6P or 5F rating. (P.B. Booth, N. Stead collection)

Dent station, May 1994. Part of the understanding with the then government for the retention of the Settle to Carlisle railway was the involvement of the private sector in the future use of the route. Here, a party of members of tourist groups are arranging future visits and discussing the use of the line in tourism ventures. One of the authors was a member of the party. (J. Marsh)

Stanier 2–6–4 No. 42648 on top of the moors approaching Dent station on the 4.40 pm Garsdale to Hellfield local train, 11 June 1960. These engines (and their Fairburn companions) were introduced by the LMS just after the war in 1945 and were based on an original 1927 design by Sir Henry Fowler. So good was this design that British Railways continued it with the 80000 series introduced by engineer R.A. Riddles in 1951. (P.B. Booth, N. Stead collection)

Garsdale station with the 'local' train from Hellifield standing at the northbound platform drawn by Fairburn 2–6–0 No. 42132, 27 August 1960. (*See* page 33). The 'local' train ran between two junction stations and at Garsdale (then in Yorkshire) the junction was with the line to Northallerton. Both Dent and Garsdale stations are in the wild moors on the high section of the Settle to Carlisle railway. (P.B. Booth, N. Stead collection)

Garsdale station with the Wensleydale branch local train at the platform waiting for passengers to stations to Northallerton, 27 March 1954. Part of the line was to close to passengers a month later and in 1959 all passenger services were withdrawn. Not only was the line then under threat but the ex-North Eastern Railway Worsdell G-5 class 0–4–4 No. 67314 must also have been reaching the end of its life as all 110 engines in this class were built between 1894 and 1901 and were being disposed of in the 1950s by British Railways. There are plans to reopen this 'Dales railway' which ran through some of the most beautiful Yorkshire Dales scenery. Rather like the Alston branch line only about a mile of the line was in modern Cumbria. (B.G. Tweed, N. Stead collection)

Kirkby Stephen main street filled with shocked mourners as the funeral cortège of those killed in the Aisgill train crash was passing to the cemetery just out of town. We illustrated the scene of the first of two fatal train crashes at Aisgill, that of 24 December 1910, on page 40 in our 1999 *Cumbrian Railways* book, but this crash happened less than three years later on 2 September 1913. Twelve passengers died in 1910 and 16 in 1913. In both crashes the train caught fire. There was, it was reported, much anger against the Midland Railway Company. (G. Dawson collection)

Crosby Garrett railway station in about 1910 had, to say the least, a rural approach road from the village. On the left can be seen the chimneys of the station building and at the far end of the lane is the goods depot. Opened on 1 May 1876, the station lasted until the 1950s. (J. Marsh collection)

Smardale on 31 July 1983 when English Electric class 40 Diesel Electric locomotive No. D200 was put on an inaugural test run from Kings Cross to Carlisle over the Settle to Carlisle track, after an overhaul. (N. Stead)

Kirkby Stephen West station in the 1960s with ex-LMS Fowler 0–6–0 No. 44277 on a southbound freight train. Designed for freight traffic in 1911, over 700 of these engines were built, this particular locomotive in 1927. (N. Stead collection)

Ormside station approach looked very tidy when this photograph was taken in about 1910. This station, like Crosby Garrett, was an early closure in the 1950s, leaving Appleby and Kirkby Stephen as the only Settle to Carlisle railway stations in the upper Eden valley. (G. Dawson collection)

Appleby West station, with the 11.55 am Hellifield to Carlisle train drawing on to the northbound platform, 23 April 1960. Fowler 2–6–4 No. 42304 was one of the first of this class of engine introduced for mixed traffic in 1927 by the LMS (the first being 42300). Note the goods yard and cattle pens on the right of the picture. (D. Butterfield, N. Stead collection)

Appleby (West) station with the southbound Waverley express at the platform, 23 April 1960. The Jubilee class 4–6–0 engine No. 45694 *Bellerophon* was of a type commenced by the LMS in 1935 at the time of the jubilee of King George V. 190 of these 134-ton engines were reported as being built up to the Second World War years and a few are recorded as being preserved following the end of steam, but this engine was not among them. (D. Butterfield, N. Stead collection)

Longmarton railway station in a photograph by Broughton of Burnley shows the station in the distance and the neat row of double-fronted railway houses, *c.* 1910. The station at Longmarton was opened in 1876 and closed in 1968. A platform-level picture of this station appears on page 45 of our 1999 *Cumbrian Railways* book. (J. Marsh collection)

Approaching the closed station at Culgaith on 11 March 1963 is British Rail 2–6–4 No. 80080 with the 'local' Carlisle to Kirkby Stephen passenger train. (*See* page 41 for further details of this design of engine reintroduced by engineer R.A. Riddles for BR, which built 154 of them.) Two of the type (but the earlier LMS Fairburn engines) were preserved by the Lakeside and Haverthwaite Railway. (N. Stead)

Langwathby Station looking south on 8 June 1965. This station was used by the Midland Railway in its Penrith and Ullswater tours (advertised on page 46 of our 1999 *Cumbrian Railways* book) as, it is said, the road to Penrith was suitable for horse carriages. The station was again used in the 1970s Dales Rail schemes. (D. Butterfield, N. Stead collection)

Little Salkeld station, as a couple wait for the train south, 19 May 1964. Situated between Langwathby and Lazonby in the Eden valley, this was a far different scene than that to be found at the stations beyond Kirkby Stephen although the attractive Midland railway architecture is evident and the Little Salkeld viaduct close to the station adds to the view when seen from the station. (D. Butterfield, N. Stead collection)

Lazonby station as the Carlisle to Kirkby Stephen 'local' train pulls to a halt, 11 March 1963. Hauling the train is a very neat looking British Rail 2–6–4 T No. 80080. This design of engine first appeared on the LMS in 1927 and the design was continued into BR days by engineer R.A. Riddles. (N. Stead collection)

Carlisle Citadel station with an ex-Midland Railway Fowler 0–6–0 No. 43922 on shunting duties. Introduced on to the Midland Railway in 1911 by Sir Henry Fowler these engines proved so useful that many survived into British Rail days. This engine is an early Midland one but its tender is from LMS days after 1923. (N. Stead collection)

Armathwaite, a southbound passenger train pulls through the station, 7 June 1965. Ivatt Mogul 2–6–0 No. 43049 is reported to have been the last of this class of engine to have been fitted with a double chimney, as was the original design. Armathwaite was the scene of a dreadful commotion during the building of the Settle to Carlisle railway when a hundred navvies confronted armed police officers after the death of an Irish labourer. (P.B. Booth, N. Stead collection)

3

The Furness Railway

Copperknob, built in 1846, was Furness Railway engine No. 3. It worked with its sister engine
No. 4 until 1898 when both were withdrawn as the oldest working engines in the country.
No. 3 was given a place of honour outside Barrow railway station in a fine glass housing (*see*
page 89) but both the housing and the engine were damaged in a wartime bombing raid.
Removed to Horwich for safe keeping, the engine became part of the national collection and
can now be seen at York railway museum, still with wartime damage.
(J. Marsh collection)

The Tuck Series No. 19 continues by showing the FR train at the beginning of the twentieth century with a Sharp, Stewart 4–4–0 engine No. 32 hauling a train of then-modern passenger carriages. (J. Marsh collection)

The Furness Railway commissioned Raphael Tuck & Sons to produce a set of postcards showing its rolling stock, etc. Here, in Series No. 18, can be seen one of the two engines in Class A2 of 1846 with a group of six four-wheeled passenger carriages. (J. Garbutt collection)

Sir James Ramsden's own saloon was built in Birmingham in 1865 and included an open veranda. It is reported that its ride on only four wheels was so uncomfortable that it was later used as an engineers' inspection carriage.
(J. Garbutt collection)

The Duke of Devonshire had his own private saloon built in about 1853. The design was intended to mimic the old stagecoaches but was so uncomfortable a ride that it was abandoned in the early twentieth century. (J. Garbutt collection)

The FR were early users of steam-driven rail-motor trains. In 1905 two were built at Barrow for use on the Coniston and Lakeside branches. Both trains had four-wheeled trailer cars for third-class passengers. Here we see a motor unit with a trailer. The entrance to the main unit was via a passage with retractable metal gates on either side. It is reported that one of the units was soon written off in what R.W. Rush described as a 'hushed-up encounter with a buffer-stop'. (J. Garbutt collection)

Furness Railway.

DATES OF OPENING·

MAIN LINE.

Year.		M.	C.
1846	Dalton to Kirkby	6	69
1847	Roose to Barrow, Old Passenger Station	1	33
1848	Kirkby to Broughton	3	43
1849	Ravenglass to Whitehaven	16	61
1850	Foxfield to Ravenglass	17	45
1851	Lindal to Dalton	1	53
1854	Ulverston to Lindal	2	68
1857	Carnforth to Ulverston	19	35
1867	Millwood Junction to Dalton Junction	0	33
1873	Barrow, Old Station, to Ormsgill Junction	1	70
1881	St. Luke's Junction to Barrow Docks	1	42
1882	Barrow and Park Loop (Salthouse to Park)	5	41
		79	33

BRANCH LINES.

		M.	C.
1846	Goldmire Junction to Piel Pier	6	13
1859	Broughton to Coniston	8	67
1863	Hawcoat Branch	0	52
1865	Millom to Hodbarrow	1	49
1867	Crooklands to Stainton	1	56
1869	Levens Junction to Greenodd Junction	0	29
1869	Ulverston to Lake Side	9	38
1873	Salthouse Junction to Stank	1	74
1876	Arnside to Hincaster (Kendal Branch)	5	25
1882	Oak Lea and Goldmire Junction	0	31
1883	Plumpton Junction to Bardsea (Priory Station)	2	0
1901	Loco. Junction to Ramsden Dock (South Side)	1	9
1906	Cavendish Bridge Junction to Pulp Works Sidings	1	6
		40	49

JOINT LINES.

		M.	C.
1855—1879.	L. & N.W. and Furness Joint Line	34	24
1867	(F. & M. Joint) Carnforth to Wennington	9	50
1880	Carnforth, F. & M. Curve	0	21
		44	15
	Total	164	17

STEAMERS.

1859 Coniston Steam Yachts
1871 Windermere Steam Yachts
1901 Barrow to Fleetwood Steamers

1846 Furness Abbey Hotel.
1910 George Romney's Early Home (1742—1755) Barrow-in-Furness.

General Manager's Office,
Barrow-in-Furness. July, 1912.

As ever, the FR General Manager, Alfred Aslet was keen to publicise the activities of the railway. Here we have a concise history of the company to 1912 to satisfy the enthusiasts, showing dates of opening the various lines, etc. (J. Garbutt collection)

SOUVENIR

OF THE VISIT
OF THE

MANITOBA TEACHERS

FURNESS ABBEY.

TO THE

ENGLISH LAKE-LAND,

TUESDAY, AUGUST 23rd, 1910.

····

With the Compliments of
ALFRED ASLETT, Secretary and General Manager,
FURNESS RAILWAY,
BARROW-IN-FURNESS.

Teachers from Manitoba, Canada visited Lakeland in August 1910 and again Alfred Aslett seized the opportunity to advertise the Furness Railway. A special eight-page pictorial brochure with itinerary for the day was given to all delegates. (J. Garbutt collection)

Included in the Manitoba brochure was a full-page copy of a then-current advertising postcard. Noticeably, Aslett's name appears beneath the picture. Our 1999 book *Cumbrian Railways* includes another of this type of advertising. (J. Garbutt collection)

Ulverston-based *Mackereth's Furness Yearbooks* featured photographs of four senior members of the FR staff, seen here and opposite. Such was their importance in the Furness area. Sir James Ramsden (top left) had steered the company from its inception in 1846. His son, F.J. Ramsden (opposite, top) became Superintendent of the line. From 1897, Alfred Aslett (top right) was secretary and General Manager. Henry Cook (left) later took on the role of Secretary. (J. Garbutt collection)

It was apparently left to the ordinary members of the Furness Railway staff to have their own photographs taken. Here we see the result when two proud members visited the studio of Shirtliffe John Priest at 22 Paxton Street, Barrow-in-Furness, opposite the Town Hall. (J. Garbutt collection)

EVERY SATURDAY,

Commencing October 1st, and until further notice,

A Special Day Excursion

WILL BE RUN TO

PRESTON, LIVERPOOL

(LIME STREET) AND

MANCHESTER

(EXCHANGE) AS UNDER :—

		a.m.	Return Fare -Third Class.		
			Preston	Liverpool	Manchester
BARROW	dep.	8 0	8/3	12/6	12/9
DALTON	,,	8 10	7/6	11/9	12/-
ULVERSTON	,,	8 25	6/9	11/-	11/3

Passengers return same day from Liverpool (Lime Street) at 10-10 p.m., Manchester (Exchange) 10-20 p.m., and Preston at 11-35 p.m.

For conditions and further information see detailed Handbills

A Furness Railway advertisement shows competitive rates for 'Special Day Excursions' to major Lancashire towns early last century. (J. Garbutt collection)

THURSDAY, MAY 17th, 1917.

DOWN.				1 Pilot Engine	3 Private Special	5 Pilot Engine	7 Private Special	9 Empty Train
				a.m.	a.m.	p.m.	p.m.	p.m
Lancaster		depart		8 53	9 8	......	......	......
CARNFORTH, L. & N.W. ...		pass		9 3	9 18	......	......	......
GRANGE		,,		9 17	9 32	......	......	......
ULVERSTON		,,		9 30	9 45	......	......	......
Furness Abbey		{ arrive		9 45	10 0	—	—	......
		{ depart		9 46	10 13	1 15	1 30	......
BARROW CENTRAL		arrive		9 51	10 20	1 22	1 37	......
ASKAM STATION		pass		—	—	1 32	1 47	......
MILLOM		,,		To arrive Shed	Empty from Furness Abbey	1 50	2 5	......
SELLAFIELD		,,				2 20	2 35	......
WHITEHAVEN { CORKICKLE ...		,,				2 43	2 58	......
{ BRANSTY ...		,,				2 46	3 1	......
Workington, L. & N.W. ...		{ arrive				3 0	3 15	—
		{ depart				—	—	3 25
MARYPORT		{ arrive				To Siddick	......	3 36
		{ depart		......	......		......	3 38
Brayton Junction		arrive		......	......		......	3 55

1 and 3 Specials—3 Engines to leave Carnforth Shed for Lancaster coupled at 7-30 arriving at 7-40 a.m. The 2 Train Engines to be leading, Tender first, with Pilot Engine in rear, also Tender first, from Carnforth. Locomotive Inspector, Inspector Culley, and Guard Benson to travel with these Engines.

5 and 7 Specials—Empties from Barrow Central at 12-35 arriving at 12-45 p.m. The Train must be drawn by the Pilot Engine and assisted in rear by the Train Engines.

Guard Benson to work 3 Special, and Guard Norman to work 7 and 9 Specials.

Engines of 7 Special to leave Brayton for Barrow Shed at 4-45, passing Maryport at 5-0, Workington at 5-15, and Whitehaven, Bransty, at 5-30 p.m.

The Royal visit to Furness on Thursday 17 May 1917 was carefully planned. Here we see the itinerary for the day with engines and staff specified. (J. Garbutt collection)

The Royal train is seen here leaving the Arnside viaduct travelling towards Penrith via Carnforth. The journey, which was a joint venture between the Furness and London & North Western Railway Companies, started at Glasson Dock near Lancaster at 8.30 am and arrived at Brayton junction near Maryport at 3.55 pm. The Royal train was preceded by a pilot engine from the Lancaster shed. The Royal party in fact had left the train at Ravenglass and travelled from Muncaster Castle to Penrith by motor carriage. The train had reversed its route in order to join the Royal party at Penrith. (J. Garbutt collection)

Opposite: Arnside station is seen here in 1926 with a train of mixed passenger carriages just after the Furness Railway Company joined the LMS. FR engine 127 is renumbered 10144. The engine was withdrawn in 1930. (J.G.D. Whitaker, J. Marsh collection)

The Kent viaduct was illustrated in the FR magazine Vol. II No. 6 of April 1922 where readers were shown this interesting comparison between the old and new columns. The viaduct was built as a single line in 1857. It was widened to a double line in 1863 and in 1887 the original cast-iron girders were replaced with wrought-iron girders supported with 10 in diameter cast-iron hollow columns. In 1910 it was noticed that some of these columns had become so soft that nails could be driven into them with a small hammer. The company decided to avoid traffic interruption and built stone piers around the existing columns. (J. Garbutt collection)

'Train Time at Arnside' by J.D. Wilson of Arnside shows a FR passenger train headed by a 4–4–0 engine with a gang of workmen on the northbound track, c. 1910. Recent refurbishment of the station has included repainting the footbridge. (J. Marsh collection)

Raphael Tuck of London produced a series of advertising postcards for the Furness Railway in about 1905. The well-known Cumbrian artist Alfred Heaton Cooper painted this view of Arnside for sale at Arnside in Series No. 8. (J. Marsh collection)

Arnside viaduct in the 1920s shows an interesting comparison between a Class M1 engine and an earlier K Class. (J. Marsh collection)

Proud FR staff assembled outside Grange-over-Sands station, *c.* 1905. One can but wonder what extra duties were carried out then, that require so many fewer staff today. (J. Garbutt collection)

Platforms at Grange-over-Sands with a crowd waiting for the southbound train, early 1900s. On the left is a slip-coach which passengers for Grange had boarded to be released from the non-stop express opposite to Holme Island, then to freewheel down to Grange station, controlled by the guard in the front-end compartment. (J. Marsh collection)

A late nineteenth-century view of Grange-over-Sands station in the days before the building of the promenade and in the early days of telegraphy – see the poles on the embankment. The southbound passenger train of four-wheeled coaches hauled by an early Sharp, Stewart engine indicates an 1880s date. (J. Marsh collection)

Grange promenade had been completed when this Furness Railway train was photographed in about 1910. The coaches, in blue and cream livery, pulled by a rebuilt 0–6–0 Sharp, Stewart engine must have been a sight to behold. (J. Marsh collection)

The line at Grange-over-Sands with Sharp, Stewart class K2 4–4–0 No. 36 drawing a train of Furness Railway late 1880's coaches. This stretch of line skirting the sea is as fine as any in the country. (J. Marsh collection)

Rebuilt Sharp, Stewart No. 34 draws into Kents Bank station, *c.* 1910. The engine was withdrawn in 1927 having LMS No. 10139. (J. Marsh collection)

This view of Kents Bank station shows the signal box which at one time was at the south end of the southbound platform. (Publisher Furness Railway, J. Marsh collection)

Kents Bank station with one lady passenger attended by three members of the FR staff. The station is little changed today except for the number of staff, being now an unmanned halt. (J. Marsh collection)

Cark-in-Cartmel station published by Frith & Co., *c.* 1900, shows the Duke of Devonshire's home station, Holker Hall being nearby. Passengers had to cross the line by the crossing seen in the centre of the picture. A footbridge was installed in 1908. (J. Marsh collection)

The staff at Cark railway station pose as a goods train passes by, late nineteenth century. All would be trained to doff their hats when their company chairman, the duke, arrived. (J. Marsh collection)

Cark railway station goods siding saw frequent transport of horses from the stables of Mr G. Dickinson of Cark. In our 1999 volume we showed a picture of August 1914 where many of his horses were being sent to the war. A month later, here is another fine group off to join the Leeds Cooperative Society. (J. Marsh collection)

Cark railway station where an excavation to install a gas supply or perhaps replace a water main draws the attention of some of the local population. The ten-man team of workmen pause for the photographer. (J. Marsh collection)

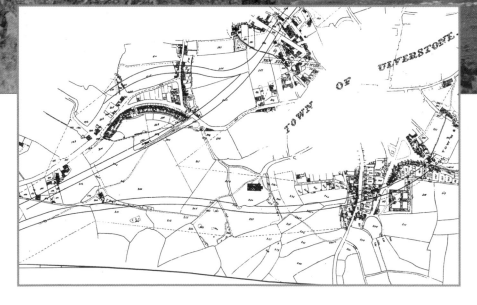

From the days of 'railway mania' comes this map by John Harris and Job Bintley, civil engineers of Kendal, who in 1845 surveyed and planned a railway from Ulverston to Windermere. They did not seem to have any regard for existing property, since the intended track ran through the centre of Ulverston and along the eastern shore of Windermere Lake. *See* page 140: 'the line that never was'. (J. Garbutt collection)

The Leven viaduct in August 1962 supports the 3.50 pm Carnforth to Barrow 'Furness Flyer' consisting of eleven coaches drawn by a Stanier 8-F 2–8–0 No. 48151. It makes an interesting comparison with the size of today's trains. (N. Stead)

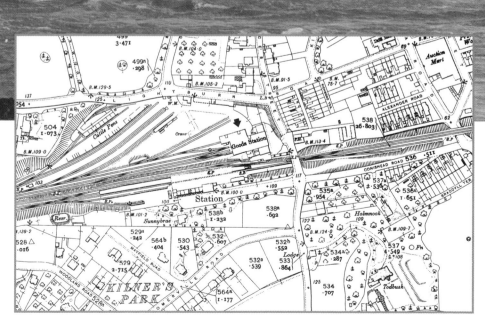

The Ordnance Survey map of 1911 shows the Ulverston railway station and goods yard in their heyday. The building marked Goods Station (arrowed) started as a passenger terminus on the line from Barrow until the main line was taken through to Carnforth in 1857. (Ordnance Survey.)

It is interesting to compare the platforms below and the goods yard above with the layout of Ulverston station shown on the Ordnance Survey map on p. 67. It is a much changed scene today. (J. Marsh and J. Garbutt collections)

Lindal station as it appeared in Furness railway days has now completely disappeared. John Linton's handbook to the Furness railway in 1852 says 'About two miles beyond (Dalton) after passing through a tunnel about 600 yards in length we arrive at Lindal, the present terminus of the railway; and here we are in the very centre of the iron district, which occupies a space of many miles in extent. . . . The line is now in course of construction to Ulverston, nearly three miles beyond Lindal.' (J. Marsh collection)

Furness railway advertising among the crowds at Blackpool was in the form of a handcart on which the round tours of the Lakes were featured, using the railway steamers to Barrow from Fleetwood. (J. Marsh collection)

FURNESS ABBEY HOTEL,

Within 1½ miles of George Romney's Home. 1742-55.

The CENTRE FOR LAKE-LAND,

One of the Ideal Hotels of the United Kingdom

OPEN TO NON-RESIDENTS.

The FAVOURITE RESORT of the ARTIST, ANTIQUARY, and Lover of the PICTURESQUE.

BEAUTIFULLY SITUATED WITHIN THE GROUNDS OF *Furness Abbey*

AND COMMANDING A SERIES OF UNIQUE VIEWS OF THE RUINS.

"The Abbot's Room."

A sitting-room called "The Abbot's Room," with ecclesiastical stained-glass window on the first floor, the celebrated *bas-reliefs* originally in the Abbey being the principal features of the room

HANDSOME LOUNGE and INGLE NOOK.

Perfect Sanitation.

Week-end Terms at Furness Abbey Hotel, from Dinner on Saturday Evening to Breakfast on Monday Morning, all inclusive, £1 5s.

THE ABBOT'S ROOM.

Adjoins Furness Abbey Station by Covered Approach.

THROUGH CARRIAGES Daily to and from the Furness Railway with LONDON, PRESTON & LEEDS.

For further particulars apply to Mr. A. A. Haynes, Superintendent of the Line, Barrow, and all Station Masters on the Furness Railway; also at Messrs. Thos. Cook & Son's Offices.

HALL & INGLE NOOK—FURNESS ABBEY HOTEL.

GEORGE ROMNEY'S HOME, 1742–1755,
BARROW-IN-FURNESS

Restored by the Furness Railway Company in 1909.

1½ miles from Furness Abbey. 1¾ miles from Barrow Central Station

One of the Greatest Attractions in the North-West of England.

NEW PAVILION within the Grounds.

OPEN DAILY, including SUNDAYS, during the Summer for Luncheons, Teas, and Refreshments

More FR advertising appeared in their many guides. Above we see the Furness Abbey hotel which was close to the residence of Sir James Ramsden, the company chairman (the hotel appears in more detail on pages 72–74). (J. Marsh collection)

Furness Railway

GEORGE ROMNEY'S EARLY HOME
(1742-1802.)

BARROW-IN-FURNESS.

(diagonal overlay:) NEW REFRESHMENT PAVILION WITHIN THE GROUNDS (under the Management of Spiers & Pond, Ltd.)

(diagonal overlay:) COACH SERVICE between Barrow Central and Furness Abbey Stations and Romney's Home: Barrow (Central), dep. 11-10 a.m., 1-15 p.m. & 4-50 p.m. Furness Abbey, dep. 2-55 p.m.

Charge for Admission to the "Home" and Grounds, 1d. each person.
Holders of Railway and Steamer Tickets admitted free.

The Grounds surrounding the "Home" have been
considerably extended.
Open Daily (including Sundays) all the year round.

— MAGNIFICENT VIEWS. —

Within 1½ miles of Furness Abbey Hotel.
Within 1¾ miles of Barrow Central Station.

TOUR No. 20.
NEW RAIL AND COACH TOUR—
GEORGE ROMNEY'S EARLY HOME
FURNESS ABBEY, WALNEY BRIDGE
AND WALNEY ISLAND,
Daily to 30th September, 1912.
(Sundays excepted).

For further particulars see other Announcements.

Barrow-in-Furness,	ALFRED ASLETT,
June, 1912.	*Secretary & General Manager.*

(OVER)

George Romney's early home was refurbished by the Furness Railway Company in 1909 and was advertised by Alfred Aslett in June 1912. Of interest is the admission charge of 1*d* per person with railway and steamer ticket holders admitted free. (J. Marsh collection)

The opening of the Ulverston & Lancaster Railway in 1854 was celebrated by a '*déjeuner*' in Furness abbey ruins and in due course the engraving for the national press report was reproduced on a postcard. (J. Marsh collection)

The Furness Abbey Hotel was (to quote the Furness Railway advertising) 'centre for the English Lake District'. Most of the building was demolished after the Second World War. (Raphael Tuck, J. Marsh collection)

The Furness Abbey Hotel series by Raphael Tuck (No. 16) included a number of views of the interior: above we see the veranda and, below, the drawing room. (both pictures J. Marsh collection)

Tuck's series of photographs of Furness Abbey Hotel interiors continues with the coffee room (above) and the Abbot's room (below). There were many abbots at Furness Abbey before the Reformation but none ever stepped inside this room, as far as is known. (J. Marsh collection)

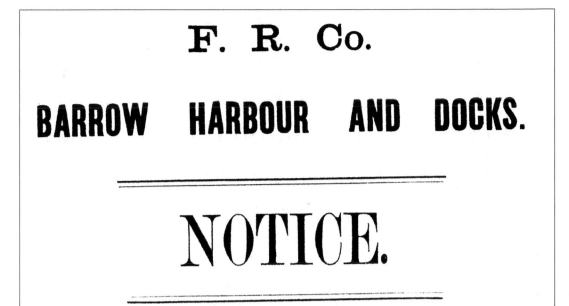

F. R. Co.

BARROW HARBOUR AND DOCKS.

NOTICE.

Whereas great damage is done to the Buoys belonging to the Approaches and Channels of Piel and Barrow by Masters of Vessels fouling them, and not reporting the same; their attention is hereby called to the Merchant Shipping Act, Section 414, which enacts that if any person wilfully or negligently makes his Vessel fast to or runs foul of any lightship, buoy, or beacon, he shall, in addition to expenses of making good the damage, incur a penalty n.e. £50.

The Master of the Schooner "Beatrice," of Barrow, was fined 5s. and costs for making his Vessel fast to No. 3 Black Buoy in Walney Channel, on the 9th August, 1882.

BY ORDER.

Harbour Office, Barrow,
12th September, 1882.

Barrow Harbour and Docks were the continuing responsibility of the Furness Railway Co., as this official notice of 1882 shows. Publicity for offenders in a 'name and shame' exercise was assured. (J. Garbutt collection)

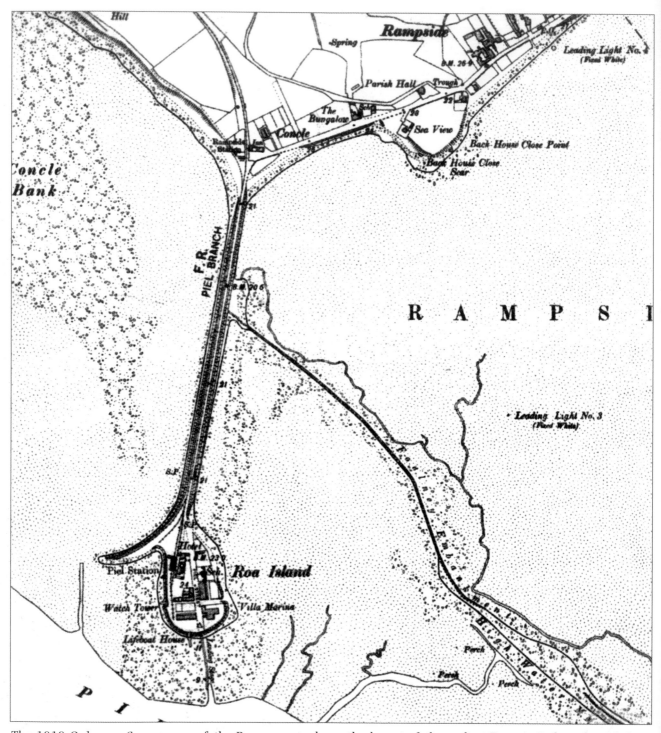

The 1919 Ordnance Survey map of the Barrow area shows the layout of the earliest Furness Railway branch line, which terminated at Piel pier on Roe Island. John Linton's handbook of 1852 tells us 'the pier was completed in 1847' and 'steamboats ply regularly between Piel and Fleetwood in connection with trains to and from Preston &c., and between Piel and Poulton, or Morecambe harbour as it is now called, in connection with trains to and from Lancaster &c. By the latter route a considerable interchange of commodities is already carried on between Belfast &c., and Yorkshire.' No doubt the FR directors of the time noted this as they pursued the extension of their railway into Carnforth and Lancaster in the 1850s. (Ordnance Survey, J. Garbutt collection)

Piel harbour station photographed from the watchtower in the late nineteenth century. This rudimentary station was obviously administered on a 'local' basis as there seem to be few facilities for passengers. *See also* page 75 of our 1999 *Cumbrian Railways* volume. (J. Marsh collection)

Ramsden dock station pictured in the earlier years of the twentieth century with a pristine FR 4–4–0 engine at the platform. This was then the terminus for the Manx steamers. (J. Garbutt collection)

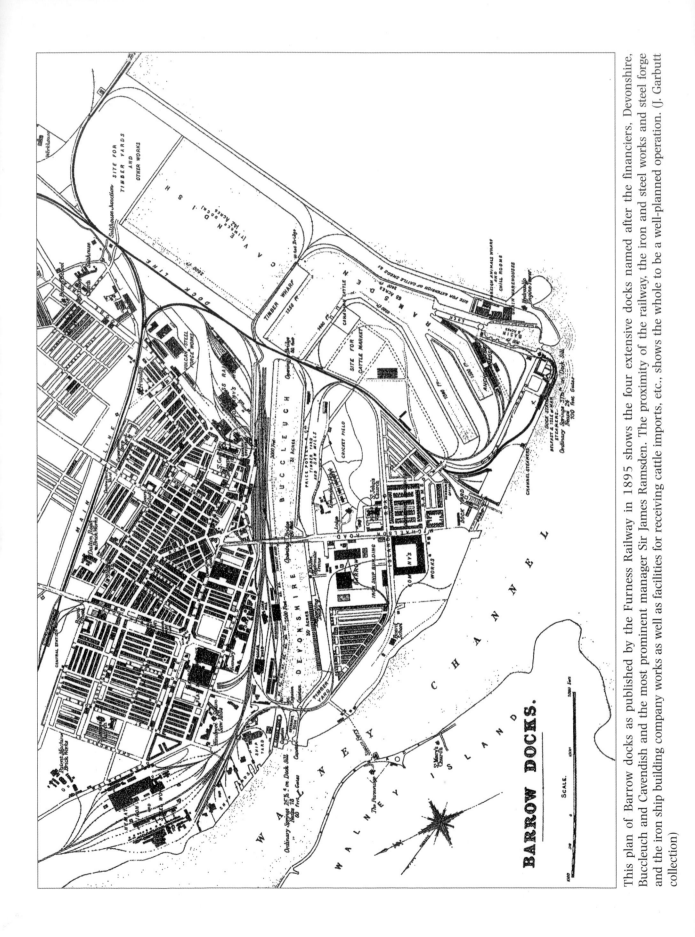

This plan of Barrow docks as published by the Furness Railway in 1895 shows the four extensive docks named after the financiers, Devonshire, Buccleuch and Cavendish and the most prominent manager Sir James Ramsden. The proximity of the railway, the iron and steel works and steel forge and the iron ship building company works as well as facilities for receiving cattle imports, etc., shows the whole to be a well-planned operation. (J. Garbutt collection)

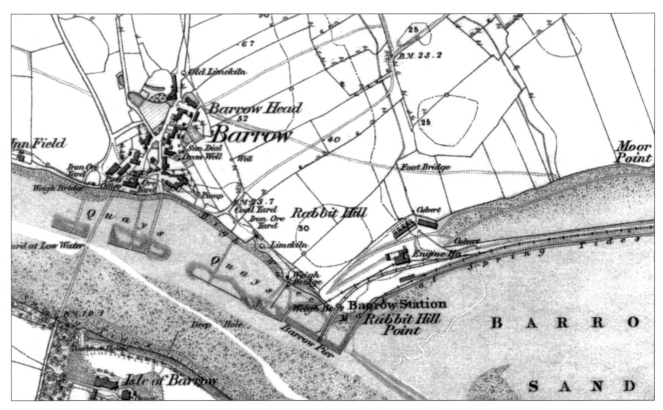

This first edition Ordnance Survey map of 1847 gives an interesting comparison with the map on page 78 showing the rapid development of Barrow in 48 years. Barrow railway station on Rabbit Hill Point and adjacent to Barrow pier was the terminus of the Furness Railway at the time. (J. Garbutt collection)

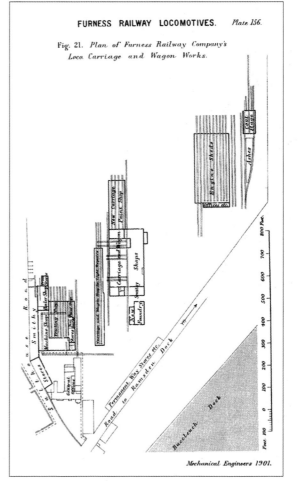

The *Proceedings of the Institution of Mechanical Engineers* of 1901 included a section on Furness railway locomotives with Fig. 21 illustrating a plan of the FR's loco, carriage and wagon works on the side of the Buccleuch dock. (J. Garbutt collection)

The interior of the chill rooms associated with the dockside slaughterhouses is also illustrated in the 1895 'Docks at the Port of Barrow' collection. Remarkably the railway siding ran directly through the facility. (J. Garbutt collection)

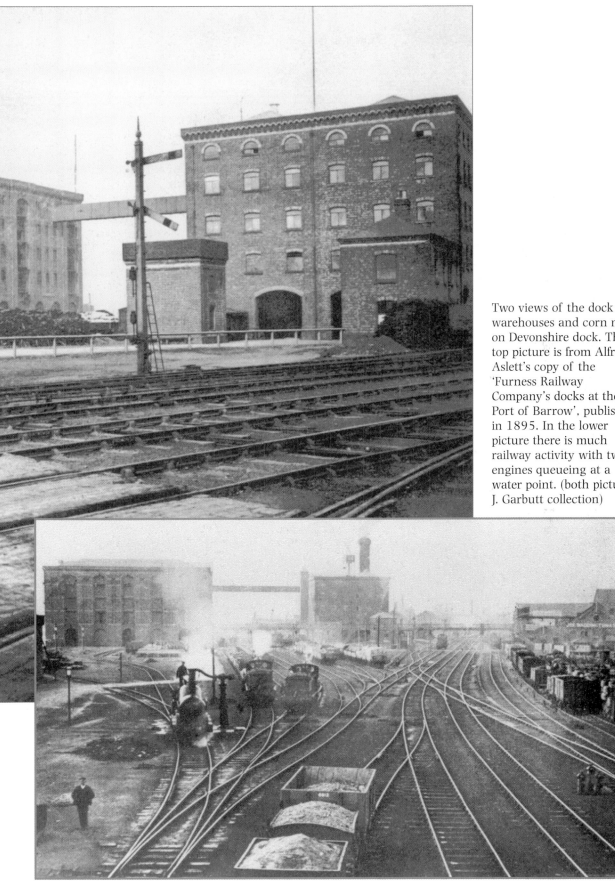

Two views of the dock warehouses and corn mills on Devonshire dock. The top picture is from Alfred Aslett's copy of the 'Furness Railway Company's docks at the Port of Barrow', published in 1895. In the lower picture there is much railway activity with two engines queueing at a water point. (both pictures J. Garbutt collection)

PS *Lady Moyra* was for many years the pride of the Furness Railway paddle steamer fleet. It provided 'an important connecting link between Blackpool and Barrow and the English Lakes'. This photograph appears in the Raphael Tuck postcard series No. 20 for the Furness Railway Co. Above we see the extent to which the boats were overcrowded. Sankeys of Barrow had a photographer on almost every trip – this excursion being on 27 May 1912. (J. Marsh collection)

Opposite: The officers and crew of the FR paddle steamer *Lady Moyra* photographed on board by Sankey's of Barrow in 1911. Details of this photograph can be found on page 30 of our *Cumbrian Memories* book published by Sutton in 2000. (J. Marsh collection)

The *Philomel* was not the most popular of the Furness Railway steamers. It had the nickname of 'full of smell', witness the obvious black smoke issuing from the stack. She was acquired because the *Lady Evelyn* had been commandeered by the Royal Navy in 1907. The lower photograph by Sankey shows the small crowd on the front of the *Philomel* on 3 July 1909. (both pictures J. Marsh collection)

PS *Lady Evelyn* came into Furness Railway service in 1901. She was so popular that she had to be extended in length. She was taken out of Furness Railway service at the beginning of the First World War. The upper photograph again shows the extent of overcrowding and the lower, a typical crowd amidships on 18 June 1910. (both pictures J. Marsh collection)

Straw boaters or cloth caps perhaps signify the direction of travel being used either by holidaymakers from Blackpool or non-fashion-conscious stalwarts from the Furness area. The top picture shows the crowd on 29 June 1912 travelling from Fleetwood to Barrow and the lower picture taken on 7 August 1912 in the opposite direction, both on the *Lady Moyra*. (both pictures J. Marsh collection)

WEEK-END TICKETS

will be issued at about **SINGLE FARE AND A THIRD** for the Return
Journey (Minimun 10/- 1st Class, 5/- 3rd Class)

— FROM —

WHITEHAVEN (Bransty & Corkickle), MILLOM, BARROW, DALTON, ULVERSTON & GRANGE,

TO

Appleby,	Ilkley,	Southport,
Bakewell,	Ingleton,	Workington,
Bangor,	Kendal	York.
Barmouth,	Keswick,	
Barnard Castle,	Kirkby Lonsdale,	*Ayr,
Blackpool,	Lancaster,	*Balloch,
Bolton Abbey,	Lytham,	*Dumbarton,
Buxton,	Matlock,	*Dumfries,
Carlisle,	Morecambe,	*Dundee,
Chester,	Penrith,	*Edinburgh,
Colwyn Bay,	Rhyl,	*Glasgow,
Fleetwood,	Ripon,	*Gourock,
Giggleswick	St. Annes-on-Sea,	*Greenock.
Harrogate,	Skipton,	

* No Bookings from Whitehaven (Corkickle) to these Stations.

The Tickets will be issued by any Train on Saturday, and will be available for return by any Train on the following Sunday (after 6-0 a m) or Monday.

CONDITIONS OF ISSUE OF TICKETS.

Excursion tickets are not transferable and will be available only to and from the stations named upon them, and any passenger using them, on the outward or return journey, at any station short of, or beyond the station named upon them, or on any other date, or by any other train than mentioned on the Excursion bills will forfeit the ticket and be charged the ordinary fare.

The Company give notice that tickets for Excursions are issued at a reduced rate, and subject to the condition that the Company shall not be liable for any loss, damage, injury, or delay to passengers, arising from any cause whatsoever.

The Company will not be accountable for any loss, inconvenience, or injury which may arise from delays to, or detention of, passengers caused by the negligence of the servants of the Company, or by any other cause whatsoever.

The FR general manager L. Speakman issued this list of destinations for weekend tickets in a
programme of excursion bookings from 3 October 1921. (J. Garbutt collection)

'Cynicus' strikes again as he did in our 1999 *Cumbrian Railways*. Although the picture is the same the wording refers to the Millom to Barrow express, but this time there is no promise to be 'back in one day'. (J. Marsh collection)

Furness Railway tank engine No. 97 was given a number which was already in use. The original No. 97 built in 1874 was then given No. 97a. Amalgamation with LMS solved the problem. No. 97a was scrapped in 1924 while 97 was renumbered 11636 and would serve out its days until 1941. (J. Garbutt collection)

FR engine No. 123, a 4–4–0 Sharp, Stewart of 1890, became LMS No. 10134 at amalgamation, only to be scrapped in 1925. (J. Marsh collection)

Copperknob (see page 43) in its glass case outside Barrow railway station before it was bombed in the Second World War, in 1941. Later the damaged case and station were objects of wonderment for the two authors as children both aged 9. (J. Marsh collection)

Millom railway station from the church tower shows a very different vista from that seen today. The extensive goods yard is busy and a passenger train in FR livery is visiting the platform. (G. Dawson collection)

The Ravenglass and Eskdale Railway received scant mention in our 1999 *Cumbrian Railways* (page 86) but we take the opportunity to make amends in the next few pages. Above can be seen the 'Eskdale Express' of one engine and one carriage passing Stanley Ghyll Hotel at Beckfoot at the beginning of the twentieth century. (J. Marsh collection)

Things changed dramatically when the Eskdale line became a 15 in miniature railway during the First World War. Messrs Meckins of Egremont photographed a new engine with rolling stock at the Ravenglass terminus. A section of the old 3 ft gauge railway can still be seen beside the later 15 in track. (J. Marsh collection)

Goods traffic on the Eskdale railway continued after the track change. Here we see the elaborate tipping apparatus for stone traffic which delivered stone into wagons on the main line siding of, first, the Furness railway, then the LMSR. (J. Garbutt collection)

The River Irt was one of the first 15 in gauge engines on the Ravenglass and Eskdale railway. Here we see Mrs Edna Kitchin of Ulverston, who was not a tall lady, dwarfing the miniature engine on a visit to the line in 1930. (J. Kitchin, J. Marsh collection)

A goods train on the Eskdale railway in the early 1920s waits on a siding for a main line passenger train. No doubt the two railway operatives dealing with miniature rolling stock would later suffer from back trouble. (J. Garbutt collection)

A striking comparison of life on the two different gauges of 'Lile Ratty'. Above, on the miniature railway the Burton-in-Kendal church choir trip of 1931 is seen at Irton Road and, below, the early twentieth century Eskdale express is seen at Eskdale station in the 3 ft days. (J. Marsh and G. Dawson collections)

The Workington area was at the northern end of the Furness Railway. On 4 September 1960 a Cumbrian rail tour called at Workington station headed by two Ivatt Mogul class 2–6–0 engines Nos. 46456 and 46442. In this photograph the activity on the station is obvious. (P. Whiteley)

The Furness Railway coat of arms with St Mary of Furness and the Cavendish family motto was widely reproduced, as on this pot-lid. (J. Garbutt collection)

FR Class D5 0–6–0 No. 27 was another engine to be given a duplicate number to an earlier locomotive still in service. The first engine with this auspicious number was a Sharp, Stewart built in 1866 and given the number 27a in 1914 when it was replaced with the superior D5. (It was scrapped in 1918.) The LMS gave the class D5 the number 12498 in 1924 and withdrew it from service, remarkably after 27 years, in 1932. (J. Marsh collection)

4

Closed Lines Miscellany

Carlisle Citadel station in the 1960s with ex-North British D30 class 4–4–0 No. 62440 standing in the platform with the train from Hawick. This engine is of the North British Scott class but this time it was Sir Walter whose books' characters gave their names to the engines. *Wandering Willie* must have added a degree of humour to the Waverley line trains into Cumbria but, like the line to Hawick, it is now a thing of the past (G.M. Staddon, N. Stead collection)

NORTH EASTERN LINES

North British Class D34 4–4–0 No. 256 *Glen Douglas* appeared in our 1999 *Cumbrian Railways* book on page 54. This engine was seen on a Carlisle rail tour in the original photograph. The tour included part of the Waverley line and here we see it at Langholm. (P. Whiteley)

At Penton, the Carlisle to Edinburgh freight train hauled by North Eastern Railway B16 class 4–6–0 No. 61439. The B16s were introduced on the NER in 1919 and were mainly used with trains of this sort. (Photo: N. Stead)

The Waverley line left Cumbria at Kershopefoot. The upper photograph shows the goods sidings and station at that remote boundary (J. Marsh collection). In the 1960s many special trains ran over the Waverley line as its closure became more imminent. Below is such a special train at Kershopefoot hauled by a Class A4 Pacific 4–6–2 No. 60031 *Golden Plover*. (N. Stead)

Alston station as seen today with its miniature railway is very different from the station we showed on page 144 of our 1999 book *Cumbrian Railways*. (J. Marsh)

Alston station in May 1956. Above, a branch-line passenger train waits at the terminus platform. 0–6–0 J39 Class No. 64705 would normally have been used for goods trains for which they were designed in 1926 by Sir Nigel Gresley. Right, the apparent chaos at the station can be contrasted with the neatness of the forecourt and goods yard. (both pictures P.B. Booth, N. Stead collection)

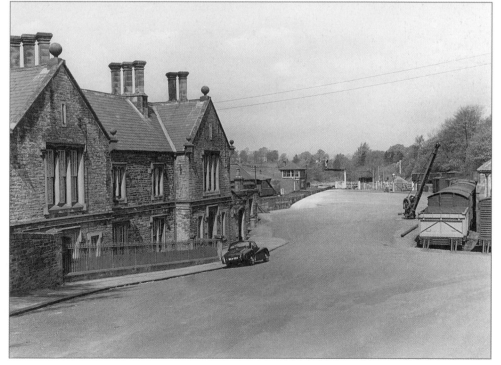

Stainmore summit with a three coach 'farewell special' train which ran on 6 May 1960, Darlington to Carlisle. J21 0–6–0 No. 65033 is shown starting off after running out of steam on the way to the summit (N. Stead)

Merrygill, near Kirkby Stephen was where a single line which ran over the Belah viaduct became a two-way track. British Rail 2–6–0 No. 77004 heads a passenger train and a signalman stands on a wooden platform to collect the single-track token. A less wary man might be in danger of losing his head! (N. Stead)

Opposite: Near Merrygill in the winter of 1955. The picture above shows the crew of a snowbound engine attempting to raise steam after the engine's failure to negotiate a snowdrift. Below can be seen a snow plough coming from the Darlington direction which was also halted by the same snowdrift. *See* page 132 of our 1999 book *Cumbrian Railways.* (both pictures J. Marsh)

The Belah viaduct. Left is a remarkable photograph from the mid-nineteenth century shortly after it had been built showing a goods train with two early locomotives and 23 wagons. This photograph was reproduced on postcards in the early twentieth century. Below is a more recent photograph showing a British Rail 2–6–0 No. 77001 hauling a Penrith to Darlington passenger train over the viaduct in the 1950s, the decade before its demolition. *See page 133 of our 1999 book Cumbrian Railways.* (both pictures N. Stead collection)

East of Kirkby Stephen east station in the 1950s with British Railways 2–6–0 No. 78011 heading an eight-coach train towards Darlington. Note that this light engine needed assistance. (N. Stead)

Kirkby Stephen east station and shed. Left is the scene in 1955 as the Darlington to Penrith train draws into the platform, where Miss Catherine Marsh is awaiting its arrival. (J. Marsh) Below is the busy scene at the engine shed on 21 May 1956 – it would surprise anyone who visits the location today. (P.B. Booth, N. Stead collection)

Kirkby Stephen east junction on the last day of operation – 20 January 1962. British Railways 2–6–0 engines Nos. 77003 and 76009 leave for Penrith on a rail enthusiasts' special. (K. Hoole, N. Stead collection)

Ravenstonedale station with a Northern Dales rail tour special at the only platform. Heading the train is an LNER J21 0–6–0 No. 65061 aided by a second locomotive LMS Ivatt Mogul 2–6–0 No. 46478. (N. Stead collection)

Gaisgill with the last-day special shown on page 115 passing through what remained of the station on 20 January 1962. (N. Stead collection)

An Ulverston to Durham miners' special hauled by ex-LMS 2–6–0 No. 46471 leaves Tebay towards Kirkby Stephen in the 1950s. (J. Marsh collection)

Tebay shed offered a range of locomotives for use, both on the line through Kirkby Stephen and the north–south main line (*see also* page 19). (N. Stead collection)

Clifton station was the first station on the North East Railway's Eden Valley line. Here the trains left the North West Railway main line after leaving Penrith. This view, showing the double track in the station (which became single track at the bridge) also includes the signal box which had not been built when the picture on page 30 of our 1999 *Cumbrian Railways* book was taken. Originally this station was called Clifton Moor but it became Clifton when the LNWR Clifton station was closed in 1938. (J. Marsh collection)

The ruins of the north-east line at Appleby are barely visible in June 1998, after the site became a scrapyard, producing piles of waste material. The platform front has been cleared away but the fine station house looks to be complete. There are plans to reopen this railway in the future, but removal of bridges would make the route on the Stainmore side of Kirkby Stephen very expensive to replace.
(J. Marsh)

The crossing gates at Appleby east station, June 1998. The line here curved away to join the Midland Railway line north of Appleby west station. Military trains to Warcop Ranges were the last to use this crossing. (J. Marsh)

Appleby station, North Eastern Railway, 5 August 1914, when the youth of Appleby, who up to then had been the Territorials at the Drill Hall, found themselves off to war. The first carriage carries the name board 'Kirkby Stephen' but the Kirkby Stephen Territorials did not leave home until 19 October. (Evans of Appleby, N. Carradice collection/G. Dawson)

Warcop station was to survive for many years after the closure of the Penrith to Darlington line as it was used by the military as part of their extensive Warcop Ranges army camp. Preston Whiteley, on his tour of closed lines in the 1960s, photographed the station before it was abandoned by British Rail. (P. Whiteley collection)

A MOD special train bound for Warcop complete with tanks and troop carriages waiting on Long Meg sidings for its right of way, 9 April 1987. It was trains such as this that kept the Appleby to Warcop line open for many years. There are plans afoot to reopen the section of track between Appleby and Kirkby Stephen as a holiday line. (N. Stead collection)

The state of the railway line between Warcop and Appleby in June 1998 can be judged from this photograph of the A66 road bridge over the line near Appleby. The lines are still present but are overgrown and neglected. (J. Marsh)

Kendal

10th Jany 1866

Dear Sir

Will you please to inform me
about what price can be got for 50 or
60, Cockermouth & Workington new £5
Shares & also for 30 or 31 £5. preference
4 1/2 % Cent Shares — and if you can give
me any information as to the position
of the Cumberland lines, as to lease
or amalgamation, Shall be obliged
I have been asked about the prospects,
I am unable to reply properly —

Yours very truly

Thos Hudson

James Irving Esq
Carlisle

Shares in railway companies were still worth consideration when Thomas Hudson, a Kendal businessman, wrote to his adviser James Irving on 10 January 1866. Today a new company is offering shares to restore a line between Penrith and Keswick. (J. Marsh collection)

Blencow station in the post-Second World War years when DMUs were used for passenger services on the CK&P. (N. Stead collection)

LMS Webb Cauliflower 0–6–0 No. 8589 drawing a passenger train near Troutbeck, Keswick in the mid-1930s. *See* our 1999 book *Cumbrian Railways* pages 137/8 for other Webb Cauliflower engines working on this line. (N. Stead collection)

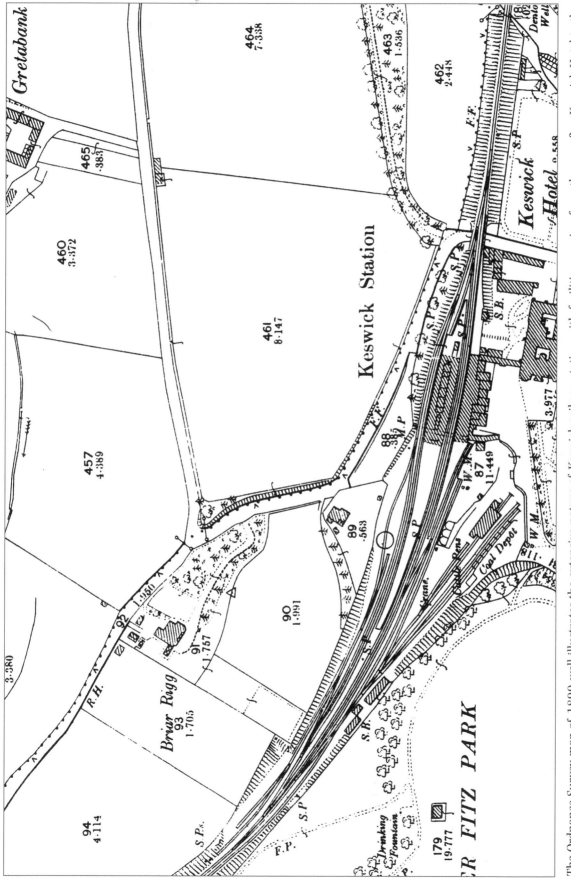

The Ordnance Survey map of 1899 well illustrates the extensive nature of Keswick railway station with facilities ranging from the very fine Keswick Hotel to the goods yard, cattle pens and coal depot. All were bordered by Keswick's beautiful Fitz park. (Ordnance Survey, J. Marsh collection)

The scene looking from platform one of Keswick station in the early 1950s shows Ivatt Mogul 2–6–0 No. 46491 standing in the platform with a passenger train. This makes an interesting comparison with the pictures below, showing the latter days of Keswick station. (N. Stead collection)

Opposite: Keswick station with a DMU pulling into platform one in the late 1950s. (P. Whiteley) Below is the same situation only a few years later, with overgrowth and neglect. (J. Marsh collection)

Keswick station seen from above in the early twentieth century, emphasising its delightful location. (J. Marsh collection)

Keswick station on 14 September 1914 with 'Keswick lads off to the front'. The war was expected to be over by Christmas so an air of excited anticipation is obvious in the young faces. The older men present, probably with Boer War experience, had a more serious view of what their leaders had in mind. (J. Marsh collection)

Opposite: Coaches outside the Keswick Hotel in 1912. Residents at the railway company's hotel had the opportunity to travel on a number of coach trips (or rounds) which took them to remote parts of Lakeland – *see* pages 2 and 4 of our *Cumbrian Memories*. The traveller who sent this postcard was French. (J. Marsh collection)

Bassenthwaite Lake station complete with road crossing and signal box. The ruins of this once busy rural station are now lost in a roadside wood. (N. Stead collection)

Bassenthwaite Lake had a boating pier adjacent to the railway station, nothing as grand as that at Lakeside on Windermere but neither were the boats. Nevertheless it attracted many tourists and locals, as can be seen in this Pettitt of Keswick photograph from about 1905. (J. Marsh collection)

Above: Brigham railway station was a junction with the Maryport and Carlisle railway with opportunities to get to many remote west Cumberland stations. (*See* pages 92 and 141 in our 1999 *Cumbrian Railways*.) Here we see Wigham Hinde seeing off visitors on the platform at Brigham in May 1963. The signal box arrived in this position in 1936. (D. Hinde collection)

Left: Brigham Bridge carried the Brigham to Bullgill line over the River Derwent. The line closed in 1935 and the bridge was dismantled in December 1936. During the scrapping of the bridge it suddenly collapsed, throwing four workmen into the river. Two drowned. Sometime earlier, Mr W. Beatty, cobbler and poet of Brigham, posed with the bridge and the Brigham to Workington line with a goods train as a background (D. Hinde collection)

Workington on 13 June 1964 as an enthusiasts' special from Penrith waits at the Main No. 2 signal box. With only two years before closure the CK&P carried many specials in its last months as enthusiasts wondered what their leaders and British Rail were up to in closing such a useful line. Ivatt Mogul 46426 (which can be seen at work with a goods train at Blencowe Limeworks in our 1999 *Cumbrian Railways*, (page 138) and 46458 haul the special through gloomy weather which probably matched the mood of the participants. (P.B. Booth, N. Stead collection)

Workington Bridge on 16 April 1966 was photographed by Preston Whiteley on his 1960s tour of closed lines. The lines curve past what had become an archaeological site for destroyed railway buildings originally built by the L&NWR. (P. Whiteley)

Workington Main was the scene of much activity when enthusiasts poured out of the special West Cumberland Rail Tour train on 5 September 1954. Aspinall ex-Lancs and Yorks Class 27 0–6–0 No. 52501 had been taken off its usual duties of shunting and goods traffic and is here seen hauling passenger stock. Originating in the 1880s, this design of locomotive lasted through the days of the LMS and British Rail up to the end of steam and a few have been preserved. (B.G. Tweed, N. Stead collection)

Moss Bay iron and steel works at Workington was the centre of much railway prosperity for many decades. In the top picture the steel works in the twentieth century can be seen along with some of the varied rolling stock that was associated with the site. Below is the ironworks, which can be seen to the right of the top picture, with the output of the railway line rolling mill awaiting transportation. The gradual closure of this heavy industry along with the iron and steel works at Barrow and elsewhere has had a great effect on the Furness and LNWR systems and closed many lines that were opened originally in the nineteenth century to service the works. Only railway line manufacture remains at Workington and that, by all accounts, is not likely to survive the international changes in the industry. (both pictures J. Marsh collection)

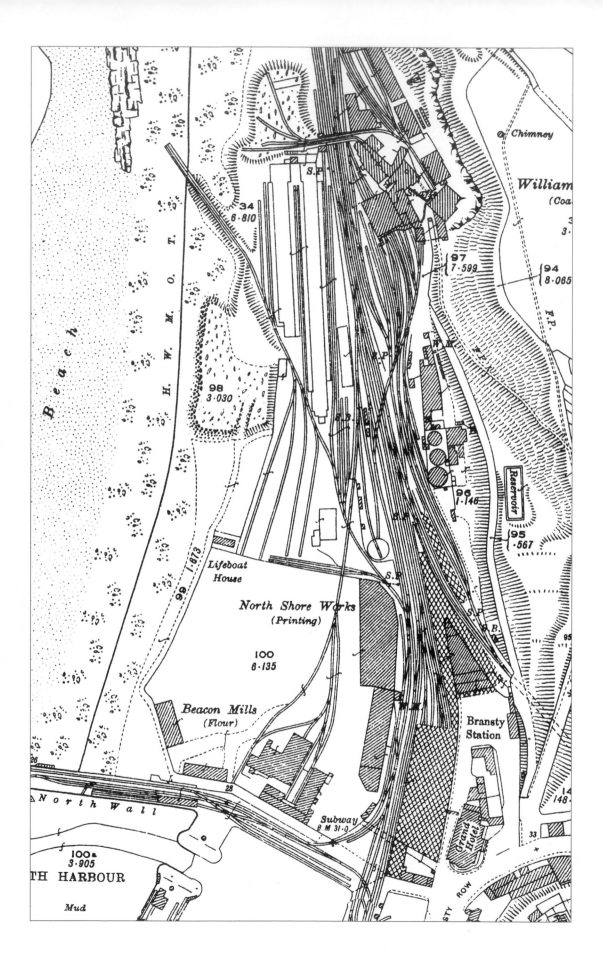

Lowgill station, 26 September 1953. This was the junction with the 'Little North Western' and the main line London & North Western Railways. Passenger trains were withdrawn in 1954 and freight trains ceased to run on the Ingleton branch line in 1965. (*See* page 97 of our 1999 *Cumbrian Railways* book for more information and pictures from this interesting and now lost branch line.) Maid of all work, Fowler 4MT 2–6–4 No. 42396 hauls a two-coach local train the year before the station closed. (B.G. Tweed, N. Stead collection)

Opposite: Whitehaven Bransty railway station. The area surrounding Bransty station with the harbour, coal mines and other industry is clearly shown in the Ordnance Survey map of 1923. Things were about to be the subject of great change as the international economic depression of the '20s and '30s took hold. The great change, as regards this book, was the appearance of the London Midland and Scottish Railway which made a start of making sense of the multitude of small railway companies which the industrial towns of Maryport, Workington and Whitehaven had had to get used to. (*See* our 1999 *Cumbrian Railways* which includes many references to the complicated west Cumberland railway system.) (Ordnance Survey, J. Marsh collection)

An enthusiasts' special leaves the Lowgill viaduct heading towards Lowgill station in the early 1960s. The engine was a development of the once famous Midland Railway Johnson Compound (examples of which we illustrated in our 1999 book). The Midland Railway use of the 'Little North Western' line and the difficulties they experienced with their competitor, the LNWR, is said to have been one of the reasons the Midland Railway constructed the Settle to Carlisle route. 4–4–0 Compound No. 41102 looks in fine form with its eight-coach 'special'. (N. Stead collection)

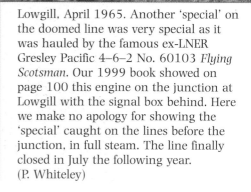

Lowgill, April 1965. Another 'special' on the doomed line was very special as it was hauled by the famous ex-LNER Gresley Pacific 4–6–2 No. 60103 *Flying Scotsman*. Our 1999 book showed on page 100 this engine on the junction at Lowgill with the signal box behind. Here we make no apology for showing the 'special' caught on the lines before the junction, in full steam. The line finally closed in July the following year. (P. Whiteley)

Below: Kirkby Lonsdale on 26 September 1953. On what must have been a gloomy journey on the local train in the year before the passenger services were withdrawn, Fowler 4 Mt 2–6–4 No. 42396 is seen at Kirkby Lonsdale station. On page 127 we illustrate the same train at Lowgill on the the same day. (B.G. Tweed, N. Stead collection)

Arnside station was the junction where the Arsnide to Hincaster branch line left the main Furness Railway line. Above is a Furness Railway 0–6–2 tank engine on the branch in 1924 – was this the *Kendal Tommy* which gave the branch its nickname? (J.G.D. Whitaker) Below is the station from the northbound main line platform with a goods train in the background on the branch line earlier in the century. (J. Marsh collection)

Arnside station with the *Flying Scotsman* attracting great attention on 2 April 1966. This magnificent engine was, for a while, at nearby Steam Town at Carnforth and any excursion caused great excitement among the rail enthusiasts. (P. Whiteley)

Sandside station with an early Sharp, Stewart/Furness Railway engine pulling a goods train along the branchline. Pages 102 and 103 of our 1999 book *Cumbrian Railways* illustrate the many changes this station witnessed over the years it was in use. (J. Marsh collection)

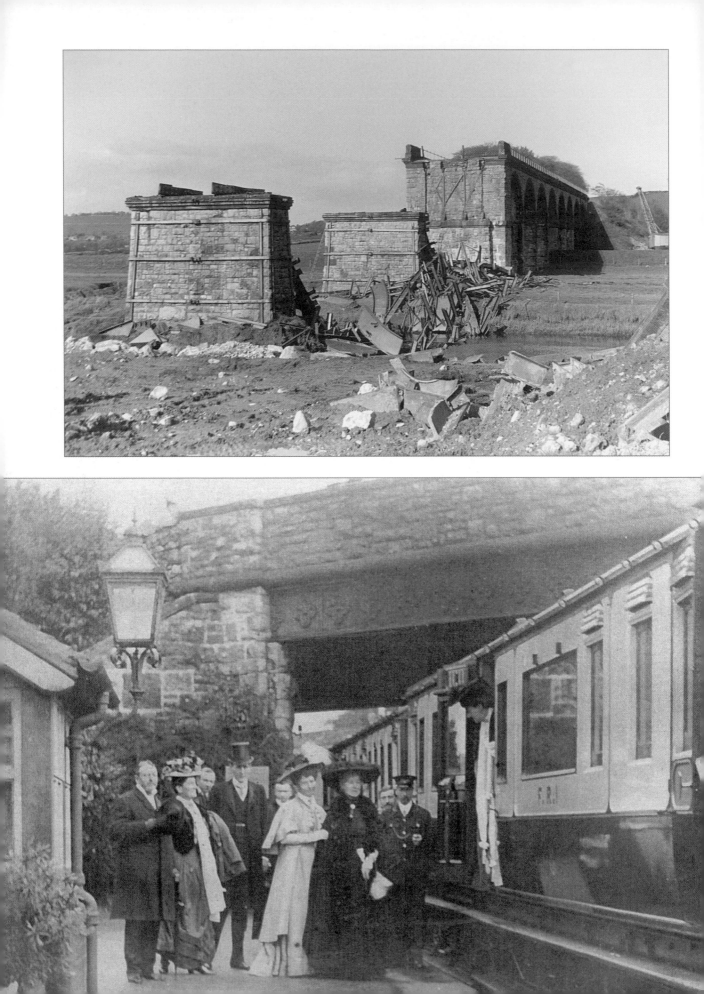

Coniston station viewed from the mines valley side with the one-carriage local train hauled by Ivatt 2MT 2–6–2 No. 41217 at the platform on 27 December 1957. 1958 saw the closure of passenger services on the branch and possibly the talk by Mr T.W. Lawrence advertised on the British Railways notice board on the right of the picture would be on this very subject. It is certain that such a talk would not include any reference to the motor vehicle pollution in the holiday months that followed the line closure. (N. Stead collection)

Opposite, top: The Belah viaduct, or Dallam Bridge, being demolished by contractors in May 1966. The speed with which this magnificent structure was reduced to rubble after the line closed caused much comment at the time, as did the inclusion of another photograph of the event included in our 1999 book *Cumbrian Railways*, which produced much interest. We are pleased to be able to include another of Preston Whiteley's series recording this destruction. (P. Whiteley)

Opposite, below: Heversham station was the scene of a Royal visit in 1907 when Princess Louise arrived on one of her many tours to be met by the Earl of Lonsdale and Furness Railway's manager Alfred Aslett. The drop to the platform must have caused some concern. (Mrs G. Carrick collection)

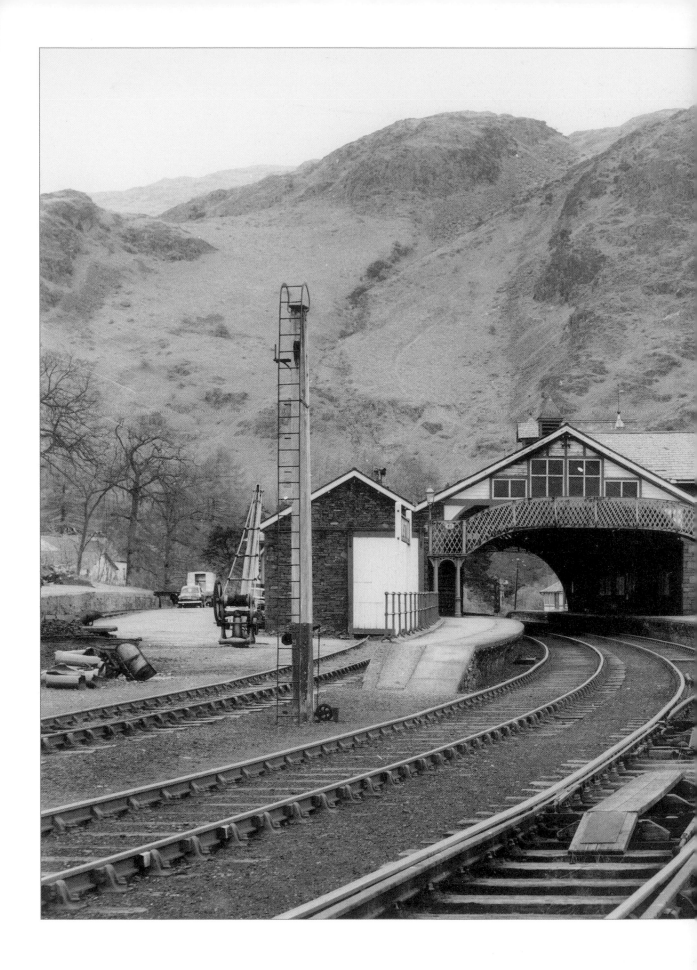

Coniston station on 24 April 1960. This picture shows what was lost when the branch line from Foxfield to Coniston was closed. It doesn't take much imagination to see what an attraction this might be today if the cuts from 1958 to 1962 had not been carried out. (N. Stead collection)

Opposite: Woodland station, 24 March 1963. The line had closed the previous year but everything looked to be in order when Preston Whiteley called on one of his tours of closed lines. The layout of this little-used station can be clearly seen as viewed from the road crossing. (P. Whiteley)

Steam Yacht *Gondola* was an attraction in its own right at the end of the Coniston branch line (although access to it from the station came as a surprise to the many who followed the railway advertising). This picture is from the Furness Railway 'English Lakes Steamers' series No. 9 which was prepared by Raphael Tuck & Sons Ltd. The *Gondola* was left to rot at Nibthwaite when the railway closed and a restoration programme (of the service but not the boat) took place between 1977 and 1980 by the National Trust. A superb replica of *Gondola* plies the lake today but none of it is original – just a wonderful replica built by apprentices at Barrow shipyard. (J. Marsh collection)

Opposite: The Steam Yacht *Lady of the Lake* arriving at Lake Bank Pier, Coniston before 1910 in the same Raphael Tuck series for Furness Railways. Many Furness railway trip passengers to Coniston found themselves on the *Lady of the Lake* instead of *Gondola*. Built in 1908 and scrapped in 1950, the *Lady of the Lake* last saw service at the outbreak of the Second World War in 1939. (J. Marsh collection)

Lakeside station was busy when this photograph was taken in the 1950s. The number of visitors travelling to the Lake District in those days using the facilities of the railways had to be seen to be believed but in spite of this the services were withdrawn and the traffic thrown on to the roads, producing the polluting congestion Cumbrians now live with each summer. (N. Stead collection)

Lakeside pier with the steam yacht *Swift* (top right) at the pier. The crowds are typical of high season in the Lake District but they did not intrude on local life as they had arrived here by train and steamer. They had not blocked the South Lakeland roads getting to Lakeside and did not leave their cars in surrounding villages and towns. Main picture: the same scene some years later from inside the station canopy with the then new MV *Swan* (2) waiting off the pier for the *Swift* to pull away. (both pictures J. Marsh collection)

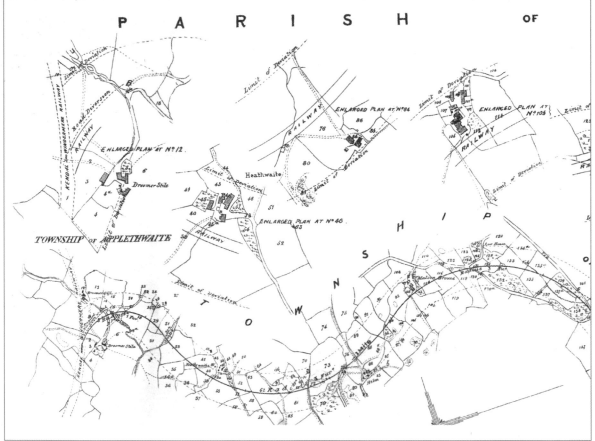

THE MARYPORT AND CARLISLE EXPRESS

The Maryport to Carlisle Railway was once a line with its own company and rolling stock but it is now only part of a track from Carlisle to Carnforth. In its early days it attracted much humour and this sort of postcard was much in demand by the holidaymakers visiting places such as Silloth. It is really a closed line even though some track is still used (as on the Lakeside branch of the Furness Railway) and the authors included it with its own chapter on page 91 of the 1999 *Cumbrian Railways* book. The postcard is by Valentine's of Dundee and dates from the early 1920s. (N. Carradice collection)

Opposite, top: Newby Bridge station was where the first rail passengers to use the Windermere steamers would alight to walk to the nearby pier near the Swan Hotel. In this picture from LMS days the station porter watches a Greenodd-bound train at the Newby Bridge platform in August 1927. The engine is of interest as it was Pettigrew, Furness Railway 0–6–2T No. 103 until it was renumbered in the LMS take over of the Furness lines. Only 19 of the class were built and the last was withdrawn from service in 1945. (J.G.D. Whitaker, J. Marsh collection)

Opposite, below: The line that never was. . . . Ulverston to Windermere was a line that was planned but never realised. The line was to leave the area of Newby Bridge and travel up the side of Windermere lake to join the Kendal and Windermere railway. We show here the planned approach to Windermere. More of the Harris and Bintley plan in the Ulverston area can be found on page 66. (J. Garbutt collection)

The sidings at Barrow-in-Furness saw the end of a series of ex-Maryport and Carlisle engines in the days following the takeover by the LMS railway in 1923. (*See* page 96 of Cumbrian Railways.) Here Maryport and Carlisle Railway 0–6–0 No. 20 awaits its fate while engines in line behind it are in the process of being dismantled. (N. Stead collection)

Carlisle to Silloth specials in the days of steam offered an escape from the workaday city life to many Carlisle folk. Here two ex-LNER goods engines (was the special as heavy as all that?) take the Silloth train near the canal junction in the 1950s. Ex-LNER J39 class 0–6–0 were designed by Sir Nigel Gresley in 1926 as goods engines but were used in British Railways days for passenger trains. Here we see No. 64733 with 64888 in front. (N. Stead collection)

Port Carlisle horse dandy can now be found in the York railway museum. We included the day that this service changed to steam on page 147 of our 1999 *Cumbrian Railways* book. Not only the youngsters liked to travel up front with the driver. (J. Marsh collection)

The Solway viaduct dated from 1869/70 and lasted until 1933. Traffic had been withdrawn about the time of the First World War because of the reduction in the iron ore traffic. This picture shows the structure in the early years of the twentieth century. (J. Marsh collection)

Silloth station in the 1950s was a busy enough place. The train to Carlisle had been reduced to a DMU and goods trains were still to be seen. Compare this view with that on page 149 of our 1999 book, *Cumbrian Railways*. British Rail did not expect the near riot that took place on the last day of operations in September 1964. Silloth as a town has been much reduced by the destruction of its railway. (N. Stead collection)

Opposite, top: Senhouse Dock at Maryport was a busy place when this picture was taken for the Valentine postcard company, in about 1900. The railway lines can be seen which would bring much traffic on to the Maryport to Carlisle railway. (Valentine and Co., J. Marsh collection)

Opposite, below: Abbeytown on the line to Silloth had its own station but who would have thought that the local postcard printers would include it, with a general view, on their postcards? (Nicholson and Cartner, Carlisle, G. Dawson collection)

The Carlisle to Silloth line can still be easily traced striding across the north Cumberland plain. This July 1998 photograph shows the route is hardly overgrown since the track was lifted in the 1960s. (J. Marsh)

Beckermet station on 2 October 1966. Compared with our picture in the 1999 *Cumbrian Railways* book page 152 we can see that the track had become a single track, that the station had been closed and was looking overgrown and the platform signal had gone. Final closure of the line was not until 1980. (P. Whiteley collection)

Moor Row engine shed on 5 September 1954 with Aspinall 0–6–0 No. 52494 waiting in steam for work. Moor Row was given extensive coverage in our 1999 book pages 150 and 151. The depot was 100 years old when the picture above was taken. (B.G. Tweed, N. Stead collection)

Egremont in the last days of the iron ore traffic. The Whitehaven Cleator and Egremont railway system dragged on into the 1980s to serve the last iron ore mine but closure really started in the 1950s when this picture was taken. 'Black Five' 4–6–0 No. 44715 takes six hoppers and a guards van by the signal box. (D.P. Leckonby, N. Stead collection)

Opposite, top: Oatlands station was on the line from Distington to Rowrah and was visited on 2 October 1966 by Preston Whiteley on one of his tours of lost railways. This desolate picture was so typical of the West Cumberland scene for many decades, the ruins of the station building being a memorial to prosperity long departed. The station finally closed in the 1920s. (P. Whiteley)

Opposite, below: Workington station on 27 July 1963 when times were a-changing. Type 2 diesel locomotive No. D5717 was photographed at Workington station with a passenger train. (P. Whiteley collection)

City of Carlisle (Stanier 4–6–2 No. 46238) was illustrated in the first picture in chapter one of our 1999 book, *Cumbrian Railways*. Then it was seen standing in Carlisle station. To conclude this book we have the same engine under full power with the Perth express in 1951 at Grayrigg. An appropriate end to our pair of books about Cumbrian railways. (J. Marsh collection)

INDEX